MYSTICAL ROSES OF PEACE

by Mother Clare Watts

Other books by the author:

Giving Birth to God: A Woman's Path to Enlightenment

Mystical Roses of Peace
1st Edition, ©2011 Sophia Publishing
All rights reserved.
Printed in the United States of America

ISBN 978-0-557-98276-9

All citations of *Poem of the Man-God* provided
with permission from:
Centro Editoriale Valtortiano
I 03036 Isola del Liri (Fr) – Italia
Tel. +39 0776 807 032 – Fax +39 07776 809 789
www.mariavaltorta.com   cev@mariavaltorta.com

For information, write to:
Sophia Publishing
1841 North Prospect Avenue
Milwaukee, WI 53202

Contact Mother Clare with any questions and
listen to podcasts of her teachings at:

www.AskMotherClare.com
www.CentersOfLight.org

Cover Art:
Reverend Meira Leonard

Acknowledgements

I am very grateful for all the editing and formatting help I received from Sister Camille Stikeleather, Rev Margaret Klapperich, Rev Monica Corvini, Rev Rachel Gonzalez, Rev Mary Francis Drake, Grace Tenner and Deacon Timothy Lin. I am also grateful to Rev Meira Leonard for the beautiful cover artwork, and to Odessa Cozzolino for the photography. I greatly appreciate all these generous contributions.

CONTENTS

Preface

By Reverend Cynthia Shepherd

As you open these pages of the *Mystical Roses of Peace*, you hold a treasure in your hands that has the potential to open your heart, mind and your very being more profoundly than you could have ever imagined. Mother Clare is a Christian Master Teacher. This book is a collection of her teachings, taken from lectures she has given to audiences across the United States over the past eleven years. Through her teachings she lays out a path and a way that is built upon love and filled with the spirit and grace of God and of our beloved Masters Jesus and Mary. It brings me great joy to know that many will be introduced to Mother Clare, to Jesus and Mary and to our Creator through these pages.

The day I met Mother Clare forever changed my life. It was the winter of 1999. I had been a seeker for some time. Though I had experienced a connection to God and Jesus through my Christian upbringing, I was always left feeling that there must be something more. There had to be. I felt this nudging and urging inside, this push and longing that revolved around the light of God, and I had an intense desire to know it and experience it. I was first introduced to the concept of light through a course I took in college in which I learned about the early Transcendentalists. I even requested of my professor to do an independent study of "The Light," but I couldn't put enough of what I was discovering into words, so the study fizzled out. All I knew was that I felt a deep love inside, and something was clearly moving me in my consciousness and experiences. I felt love as a small child learning of Jesus through hearing the parables and through taking my first communion. What I saw and experienced in the world presented such a deep contrast to those inner feelings that I couldn't make sense of it or understand what was happening in the world around me or inside of me. Questions and confusion arose within me and passed through my heart, leaving me feeling a deep hunger. The longing and desire to experience more deeply this light of God was a prayer deep in my heart that was seen and heard and recognized by Mother Clare in my very first meeting with her.

That meeting is forever impressed upon my soul. My heart leapt to finally encounter someone who knew exactly what I was seeking and how to lead me there. I told her I wanted to know and experience the love and light of God, to really know it. She looked right into my eyes, through my being and I knew she had that connection, that knowing and experience of God that I had been longing for. I felt as though my heart, my mind, and my soul were being seen for the first time. She was simple, loving and clear and gave me the first steps to take. In the days, months and years that followed, this desire for the light and love of God led me into deeper experiences and lessons than I could have ever imagined.

This collection of Mother Clare's teachings and wisdom, *Mystical Roses of Peace*, is truly a bouquet made of the purest consciousness, integrity and love of Jesus and Mary. Each chapter is a perfect flower, different in beauty and scent, a lesson unto itself where she opens the deepest recesses of your heart, touching into your soul's longing and desire for connection with God. She speaks right to the heart of human brokenness and pain and then steadily guides you through the steps of finding a teacher and how to open to these teachings and love. Ultimately, she lays out the steps one must take to come into total union with God and how to live in that consciousness always. You, the reader, have the opportunity to most beautifully experience Mother Clare's fire and intensity as a teacher of truth and, at the same time, to get wrapped in her very tender consciousness and love that knows the wounds and pain of the human heart and condition. The love of Jesus and Mary pour through these pages. Their love is in each nuance, each expression and each word.

If you have a spiritual longing, a hunger for peace and consciousness, and a desire for God you are about to receive a great gift. May these lessons awaken your soul's longing to grow. May they help you to find a teacher of your own and may you follow him or her to the ends of the earth and into the realities, consciousness and love of the spiritual world.

In her chapter, "Giving of Yourself" Mother Clare says:

"Real spiritual teachers have no motives other than to give to you the great peace that they have come to know and to bring you into living in the phenomenal experience of knowing God's Love for you as they have come to know God's Love for them. We teach because we know the way. We love because we have been loved."

May you be blessed as you open to receive these mystical roses of peace.

Introduction

By Mother Clare Watts

'The Rose is a mystery' – where is it found?
Is it anything true? Does it grow on the ground?
It was made of the earth's mould, but it went from men's eyes,
And its place is a secret, and shut in the skies.
In the Gardens of God, in the daylight divine
Find me a place by thee, Mother of mine.
But where was it formerly? Which is the spot
That was blest in it once, though now it is not?
It is Galilee's growth; it grew at God's will
and broke into bloom upon Nazareth Hill.
In the Gardens of God, in the daylight divine
I shall look on thy loveliness, Mother of mine.
What was its season, then? How long ago?
When was the summer that saw the Bud blow?
Two thousands of years are near upon past
Since its birth, and its bloom, and its breathing its last.
I shall keep time with thee, Mother of mine.

~ Gerard Manley Hopkins, "Rosa Mystica"

‍I first learned about the existence of spiritual master teachers when I was 18. I was instantly fascinated and decided that nothing in my life mattered more than to find a real spiritual teacher who could take me all the way into the heart of God. I didn't know exactly what that meant, but I felt very sure in the deepest part of my being that I needed to find a teacher and ask him or her to help me find God. For ten years, the search for my teacher led me through living in two yoga ashrams and a Sufi spiritual training school and eventually to a real teacher who was willing to teach me in the mystical Christian tradition. After 12 years of training with master teachers, during which time I served as a deacon minister, I was ordained a mystical Christian priest and began to teach others through a women's order that I founded. In 2001, I was ordained a master teacher myself. The all-women's order became a men and women's order, which I co-founded and now lead with Father Peter Bowes.

Though there are highly inspirational writings from a number of great mystical teachers throughout history, my students often find those writings don't answer their questions that pertain more to their earthly lives. How are they supposed to fit a spiritual life into an already busy schedule? How do they find the right teacher for them? How can they go deeper spiritually and give more to God? This book is an answer to many such questions. Though I am deeply mystical in my practices and orientation, I recognize that a bridge is needed between daily life issues and questions and the lofty heights of union with God. My aim is always to be of guidance and support to seekers no matter where they are along their path toward union with God.

I offer to you, my readers, these chapters as little mystical roses. The great Mystical Rose is Mother Mary, known as such by many of her devotees. My prayer is that the simplicity, clarity and purity that is so characteristic of Our Mother will come through to you as you read these teachings. May each chapter answer some questions that have kept you stumped, illuminate an issue that has long troubled you, and inspire you to keep seeking God until you find God and come into ecstatic union with that unfathomable love at the center of your being. And may you deepen in peace through the unfolding of each of these mystical roses within you.

CHAPTER ONE

Spiritual Growth and Development

*If a man should conquer in battle a thousand
and a thousand more, and another should conquer himself,
his would be the greater victory,
because the greatest of victories is the victory over oneself.*

~ Buddha, *Dhammapada*

Human beings have always had a great interest in the world of the spirit. Virtually all cultures of all times have demonstrated a striving to connect with that world and to somehow become linked to it. People sensed that through connection with the realm of spirit, they would gain the wisdom, the know-how and the power to make their lives and the lives of those around them better. Some people in each culture feel powerfully drawn to finding out how to grow and develop spiritually because they sense that they will then truly experience happiness and fulfillment – that they will know what they need to do with their lives and therefore live with a sense of purpose and mission. Sometimes we intuit early in life that spiritual growth will grant us what we seek to be and how we want to live. Sometimes we arrive at seeking such development after all else has failed us. So, you may decide to seek God and do the work to grow spiritually because you feel drawn and have a burning desire to do so. Or you may feel driven to a spiritual search because of the pain and sorrow you have experienced.

Both approaches will have served the purpose of making you begin to seek, and both will have cultivated your desire to grow.

Once you have decided that you want to grow spiritually, the next step will be to find a means to do so. You could sit and meditate for hours every day and hope that this practice will lead you into enlightenment. However, the chances of this are very slight. Many have tried, and extremely few have succeeded. Why? Because if you don't know what to do while sitting quietly and you don't know where to go with your mind, you will very likely space out or think about everything but that which was to be the focus of your meditation. Even if you could still your mind and emotions and focus, how would you know what to focus on? How would you know where inside to look and what to do in that vast inner world? Moreover, if you did make contact with some other spirit, how would you know whether it was a good spirit, someone you could trust, versus some lost being who was roaming around in the psychic realms?

The inner realms of our beings are quite vast. Our thinking and emotions have blocked our ability to delve into these inner realms. Within those realms, all the functions of our thinking and our emotions are used to running the show. The cravings of our five senses for a myriad of comforts pull on our attention. Consequently, when we go inside ourselves seeking relationship with God without a guide, it is as if we are in a foreign country whose language we do not know and whose culture and layout are unfamiliar to us. It would be as if we were looking for a particular person for whom we have no known location or address. The likelihood of us finding that person by spending an hour or two a day wandering around this vast country, even if we do it for years and years, is quite low.

So it is with the inner world. People often enter into it with great naiveté, thinking there is a small space inside of them and they will easily stumble upon God without any need for help or direction. In truth, when you try to turn your focus inward you will likely find everything but the presence and peace of God. We read and are told that if we sit on the right kind of cushion or in the right position, if we use the right incense, burn the right candles and perhaps focus on a particular Sanskrit word or sound, then we will be able to enter into the promised land of inner peace. In fact, I have never met anyone in all my years in yoga ashrams, Sufi training and Christian practices who was able to do this. Yes, many of us learned to at least still our minds somewhat. We learned to feel that there was more than what we see with our physical eyes. We got a sense that inner peace was possible, and we often found that our days went better just because we got a little quieter for a time each day. Sensing the possibility of quieting even a bit was certainly better than nothing, but it was a far cry from what we had read about and what we had hoped for.

When this has been our experience, we often do not last too long in the continuation of that practice because we sense that more should be able to be gained from it. Some people, however, are so happy for the increase of peace they obtain through such a practice that they are satisfied with it and do keep it up, sometimes for many years. But most fall away, read another book or try another way to enter into the state of union with the presence of God, which they hear is possible.

The reason why meditating in such a way is not very fruitful for most people is because if they are doing only this spiritual practice, they are missing all the other elements of what together produce actual, deep, and real spiritual growth and development. They are operating under the misunderstanding that one simply starts wherever one is and through stumbling around in the desert of one's mind one will come upon God. In fact, real spiritual growth comes about through a multi-faceted approach that involves all aspects of one's inner and outer lives. In order to actually come into the presence of God and have an open and flowing love relationship with God, a person will need to clear out the trouble and the noise from every part of their insides and outsides. Why is that? Because every aspect of your life that is unconscious, reactive, unclear or messy will get in the way of your coming to God. If you could see each of those visually, they would look like clouds of various levels of darkness that block the sun. To not address all these issues would be the same as trying to soak in the sun's rays while under a thick cover of clouds. The sun is, in fact, there within you, as you have heard. But with all those clouds between you and it, you cannot see it or even barely sense its presence. You might gather from the light that does come through the clouds that there must be a sun on the other side of the grey. However, you could not actually come into relationship with that sun except in a vague and hopeful way.

Why have you not been told this? Well, in a sense, you have. The writings and teachings of the great masters have always addressed the fact that how you lead your life externally and internally matters. They have advocated clean living, including being watchful about negative thoughts and emotions. They encouraged you to seek to hold inside your mind and heart only what is in accord with God, with light and with peace. In doing so, you are attuning yourself to that energy and hopefully increasingly entering into it over a long life of faithful practice. Now, however, we have much more direct ways to help clear those clouds that obscure our vision and our relationship with God. Growing and developing spiritually will entail giving it everything it takes to clear those clouds. You can attempt to do that by yourself – many do – but you will be like the blind leading the blind. That way of trying to progress is bound to be long and not very effective. Much more effective is the long-held practice of taking on a spiritual teacher who can see and identify the makeup and origins of those clouds in your life and knows how to dispel them. What might that cleanup look like?

The first layer of clouds that keeps you from connecting with God within is made up of your body's demands on you. When you first try to sit still, you will likely find your body wanting to distract you in various ways. You may feel itches or twitches, restless feelings in your legs or arms, a sudden need to go to the bathroom or to eat and drink. When this happens, you need to simply learn to discipline your body. Discipline is a dirty word for many people. Those who feel that way about discipline want things to be easy and pleasurable and don't want to have to discipline any aspect of themselves. You can choose to maintain that opinion, but you will never enter into those parts of yourself that hold the potential to bring you all the happiness and peace you almost gave up on. You will need to tell your body that it is not the boss of you and that right now you are going to be quiet, and you would appreciate its cooperation. Over time, your body will then settle down and you will be able to sit completely still for long periods of time. Your body will have learned to stop trying to send you distracting messages when you are meditating and will relax and support your efforts.

Once you have overcome your body's resistance to being still, you will run into the incessant noise coming from your thoughts and your emotions. Stilling the body may have been challenging for you, but stilling the mind and emotions is significantly more challenging. Why is that so? The reasons are two-fold: 1) You have allowed these two faculties to run amuck all of your life. They are like unruly children who have always had their way. Your thoughts will tend to jump from one subject to another or obsess on something once you entertain it. Your emotions are stimulated by your thinking, which in turn stirs up more thoughts, and you get caught in endless rounds. 2) The patterns of thoughts and emotions that you have were established in you as a means to cope with your life. When you were little and you got hurt and so scared by what was going on in your life, you built up places in your mind and heart where you learned to go in order to survive. Those cop-ing mechanisms may well have helped you survive childhood, and that was good. But now as an adult, you will find that when you go inside, before you can draw close to God, you will have to encounter and deal with all the hurt, angry and sad thoughts and feelings. Why? Because they form a large part of the cloud cover that keeps you from God within. Without addressing what is in your conscious and unconscious minds and what pain and fear fills your heart, you will be stuck and unable to experience the bliss of resting in God's peace.

You may wonder why God created us that way and why God doesn't just let us approach in spite of having innumerable is-sues in our minds and hearts. In fact, God did not create us that way. God created us with clear and easy access to God. It is we who built up this cloud cover because we sank ever deeper into our fear, our anger and our hurt. As we did so, we drew farther and farther away from the presence of God, and we added on layer after layer of defenses and repressions of feel-ings. This is how we arrived where we are. We hold so many concepts we believe are true that without the help of some-one who has already done this work in themselves and has learned how to dispel those clouds that keep us from God, we are highly unlikely to find our way. Some people are convinced that growth needs to be hard and slow; some believe it is best to ignore everything that is uncomfortable. Some people feel they do not deserve to be loved; others are afraid to allow love in. Some people believe that if they do not stay angry with those who hurt them, then those offenders will have gotten away with the offense; some believe they are too weak to ever stand up to abuse. We hold so many beliefs, assumptions and concepts that we are often completely oblivious they are po-tentially not true.

A spiritual teacher who has the right skills to help you through this will help you address those clouds within you. What you have so long kept repressed yet continues to bother you from deep inside and keeps you depressed, anxious, angry or afraid will ever so gently be allowed to come up in a supportive and loving environment. As each issue comes to light, it will be addressed, and through the use of various spiritual tools, it will be worked with until it is healed. The spiritual teacher will simultaneously help you connect ever more to the love and light of God as the clouds that have kept you separate clear away. You can certainly attempt to do this work without a teacher, but you will need to accept that the results will be very slow and will still, most likely, not bring you much closer to God. If knowing this, you still feel too afraid to invite a teacher to help you, you can keep working on it alone. I do, however, recommend that you examine whether your reason to want to go it alone is because you are too proud to allow yourself to be helped. Pride would be a sad reason to miss out on something as wonderful as entering into the direct and loving embrace of God.

Some of you who are already working with a teacher may find that you are not really growing as fast you would like. Why is that? The primary reasons for slow growth are: 1) Unwillingness to do the work that your teacher asks you to do. 2) Attachment to your problems and reluctance to let them go. 3) Refusal to accept that you can be whole and that you could be loved. 4) Believing your growth and healing needs to be hard and slow. Many people also do not want to grow up and be responsible, so they continue in their dysfunctional childish patterns to try to get the love they never received as a child. If you are one of the stuck or slow ones, you need to consider whether you actually want to change and become whole. If you do and you have a spiritual teacher, let your teacher point out to you what is keeping you stuck, and then jump into the transformation that is being made available to you. I guarantee you that if you do, you will look back on how long you held onto your issues and be amazed at the folly of doing so. You may feel some sorrow for all the time you wasted.

The great beings of light are looking for students who want to courageously forge ahead. If you still want to wallow in your pain, fear and anger, the spiritual path is not for you. You can hire a therapist and tell them all about your issues and keep seeing them for the rest of your life. Many of them will allow you to stay stuck for as long as you want. But with a spiritual teacher, it is different. A real spiritual teacher will pour love into you until the cows come home, as long as you are making use of it and doing your part to grow and change. But if you want to continue being stuck and babied or want to change an inch every few years, a time may come when the teacher suggests that you don't really seem to need or want their help. It may not be until you lose the teacher that you realize what you had and how little you made use of it. So if you have a teacher, I suggest you decide to grow – dynamically, swiftly and courageously – and move into the peace of the light.

Whether you have a teacher or not, I applaud all of you who choose to grow. Take the challenge and shoulder your part of the work to become shining examples and giving lights in this world of sadness and fear.

CHAPTER TWO

Will and Desire

What this power is I cannot say;
all I know is that it exists and it becomes available
only when a man is in that state of mind
in which he knows exactly what he wants
and is fully determined not to quit until he finds it.

~ Alexander Graham Bell

I have been teaching spirituality and guiding students into the inner realms for more than twenty years. As a spiritual teacher, I have the joy and the responsibility of helping students discover what prevents them from further growth and how they might overcome it. Early in my work, I began to see the truth of the Sufi teaching which states that the primary two qualities needed to grow spiritually are will and desire. When I meet with students who are lamenting the slowness of their spiritual growth, I can unfailingly see that they are lacking in one or both of these two great means to move themselves forward. These two powers are not randomly assigned to us at birth; their presence in us is not a matter of luck. We are certainly born with more and less of each, but the reason for this is not random. Rather, we came into this life with whatever strength of will and desire we developed in previous lifetimes. If before this incarnation we have already excelled at developing one or both of these, we will begin to demonstrate those strengths quite early in this life. Even small children will often demonstrate an amazing will or tenacious desire to acquire the object upon which they have set their fancy. Many parents can attest to their shock when first encountering their young child's unyielding insistence that she gets what she wants.

Let us examine each of these powers separately, so that you may obtain a deeper understanding of what they are. We will then look at how deficits in each of them manifest and lastly at how to develop these qualities into the powerful assets and tools that they are meant to be.

The American Heritage Dictionary defines "will" as the following:

1) the mental faculty by which one deliberately chooses or decides upon a course of action; volition;

2) something decided upon by a person of authority: It is the king's will that the prisoner be spared;

3) deliberate intention or wish;

4) the power to arrive at one's own decision and to act upon it independently in spite of opposition: A woman of strong will and purpose;

5) determination; diligent purposefulness; self-control; self-discipline.

These are indisputably powerful descriptions. The strength that moves through each description leaves the association of will with power beyond question. In fact, the power of the determined and directed will of a human is only surpassed by the will of God. All the technological wonders that move great energy and power are the manifestations of a person or several peoples' will and desire to create them. Therefore the presence of human willpower and the desire to create is required before any material human-made object or development can take place.

Why is will so powerful? What makes it such a force, and why does it carry so much energy? Consider where in your body you feel will originate. If you feel it is located in your head, you are referring to the will of your thinking mind. One of the forms of will is located in your head. That form arises when you decide in your mind that you want to pursue a particular action or achieve a specific goal. When you use that will, your mind stays focused and pursues the chosen course. Many choices that we determinedly follow are supported by this mental will and a desire to achieve the hoped-for results. We need a well-developed will of the mind, at least until we fully develop the other type of will, that which originates in the God-Self, which will be described in a moment. Note that this head-based form of will can also be fueled by negative emotions and can thereby bring about much trouble. For example, when Hitler decided to go on his ethnic purification rampage, that will originated in his mind and was fueled by his hatred, his anger and his desire for power. That was the immensely destructive combination he held, and his political office gave him the means by which to put his plans into action. The results were, as you know, horrifying.

The aforementioned second form of will is, however, a much more powerful form of will with which you can learn to connect. Its source lies in your torso, in the vicinity of your solar plexus. When the will behind a plan or an action is flowing from this source, you won't feel like the energy or vision is coming from your head, but you will feel more like your whole being is behind the chosen action or decision. The will that flows into you from this source, is in fact, the great will of God. Every true mystic longs for the day when they enter into the will of God, and it becomes their sole motivator and director. We come to this state of oneness with God's will through progressive steps of learning to trust God and becoming ever more willing to let go of our thinking that only we can determine what is best for us and therefore only we should be making decisions for ourselves. Mystics have given up such thinking, finding delight in flowing with the will of God wherever it may take them, knowing the outcome will always be what is best for them and for all involved.

Now let us discuss desire. According to the dictionary, "to desire" means to wish, long for, or crave. Why do we need a strong desire for God and for spiritual growth and development in order to grow? We need this desire because God will never go against what we want. God does not violate human will. If we do not want to draw near to God, God allows us the freedom to stay away. Therefore, only after we develop a desire for God can we begin our journey into the spiritual realms. If our desire for God and for spiritual growth is weak, we will want other things more than we want God. And because God gives us what we want, we will get those other things, rather than God. We will therefore need to desire to know God and be in relationship with God more than anything else in our lives in order to truly come into such relationship and such knowledge of God.

People often think they want a spiritual life, but in fact, when they examine what they want more deeply, they see that they care more about their family, having or keeping a mate, having material success or having recognition from others. The desire for God is not powerfully present from the beginning of a life on earth, at least not for most people. It grows little by little as people follow their initial hunches that they should seek out God, and then they begin to have actual experiences of God. The desire continues to grow throughout a person's life, as long as it is nurtured and developed through spiritual and devotional practices.

What then should you do if you find you are lacking in personal will, the type that comes from our thinking? We do need this form of will, and if we don't have much of it, we can choose to develop it. Often the lack of will stems from being overly picky about what you want, with overly developed peculiarities. Therefore, everything is not quite right, and as a result, you don't put your will behind bringing it into manifestation. Another block to having a strong will is laziness. When this is your situation, you allow your laziness to be the prime determinant of what you do. In such cases, you will actually use your will to support your laziness and thereby become willfully stubborn about not doing much of anything that would require you to work, struggle or stretch to challenge your body, heart, mind or soul. If this is your situation, I suggest you consider carefully whether you wish to remain stuck in your stubborn rebellion against changing and growing. You can choose to stay stuck, if you want, but you will pay a price for that. Your pain will become greater and greater over time because of your resistance to the loving presence of the spirit of growth and life, whose directives you would be refusing to receive. You may be quite proud of how stubborn you are, feeling that is the greatest power you hold. Then keep it, until you have had enough of it. You have that right.

If, however, you want to develop your decisiveness, your "power to arrive at your own decision and to act upon it independently in spite of opposition," as the dictionary describes it, you will have to decide to overcome your laziness and your pride in being able to stubbornly resist any higher will. You will need to learn to concentrate and practice making decisions and sticking to them, come hell or high water. You will need to challenge yourself by taking on ever increasing levels of commitment and responsibility and making sure you follow through. A great goal is to become a person of your word, where others know that you will do what you say you will do.

What if you seem to not have enough desire for God? If this

is your situation, you need to acknowledge that you want other things more than you want God. I suggest you then look at what those things are that you so desire, and deeply question whether they are really worth more than bringing your soul into accord with its purpose for being on earth. You are choosing those little things of earth over allowing yourself to be brought into the loving embrace of the God within you. Thinking that other things matter more is simply a misunderstanding of what will make you happy and what will bring you peace. The truth is that happiness and peace come from the deeply satisfying constant experience of God's love and protection, not from hearing about it, but from living within the reality of the experience.

What do you stand to gain if you, in fact, decide to pursue the development of your desire and will so that you can come close to God? That God within you, the one who lives in the area of your solar plexus, will begin to fill you with God's view of yourself, others and the world. You will develop the ability to see and understand things from God's point of view. Once you do, you will not want anything else because you will see the perfection of God's plan and the wisdom of God's actions. You will desire to draw ever deeper into that amazingly loving presence of God within and simultaneously allow God to come forth ever more into your whole being. And in time, you will no longer be so separate from God. Your desires will be identical to God's; your will will have given itself over to wanting only what God wants. You will be in peace and lifted up in the ecstatic embrace of divine love.

All this can be yours if you choose to enter into the mystic way of life, ever seeking the light and love of God. However, I tell you again, you do not need to do this until you want to. God is patient. Though God longs to draw you into God's ecstatic love and overwhelming peace, God will not force you. When, and if, you choose this, God will be there. May your way to God's loving embrace be blessed.

CHAPTER THREE

Finding the Right Spiritual Teacher for You

*Whoever travels without a Guide needs two hundred years
for a two-day journey.*

~ Rumi

I am aware that you, the reader, could be at any one of the many different stages of finding and following a spiritual path. You may be considering looking for a teacher for the first time. You may already be working with a teacher and are moving along the spiritual path. Some of you may have a teacher but do not feel you are moving along as much as you would like. I believe you will find yourself and your situation addressed in this chapter, and you will get a clearer picture of how to find the right teacher for you. You may also get a sense of what it might be like to work with a teacher.

What makes a person first decide to look for a spiritual teacher? Obviously, the vast majority of people do not feel that need. So where would such an idea come from within a person, and what would they be hoping to get from a relationship with a spiritual teacher? To answer these questions, I will need to give you a basic spiritual anatomy lesson. We humans have, in addition to a physical body, a spiritual body that is the same shape as our physical body. The spiritual body is within and

around the physical body, and within that spiritual body is located our soul and our God-Self. The God-Self is like a flame
within us and is a cell of pure God. It is surrounded by our
soul, which has been shaped and formed by all of our life experiences during our many lives on earth. The soul's longing
and desire is to be in a loving relationship with the God-Self
and to fulfill its mission on earth, the purpose for which it was
born. The soul has, however, become encrusted with a murky,
dark coating from all the hurts, sadness and disappointments
in life. This dark coating on the soul keeps the light of the God-
Self from shining through it.

The dark crust begins to thin out and get cleaned off through
contact with spiritual people and through consciousness-
raising activities as we attempt to become more aware and
connected to life, light and love. Spiritual readings, church
events, classes or workshops can begin to awaken the desire
of the soul to connect with God and inspire us to do what we
are meant to do in this life. When this awakening happens, we
will feel that desire bubbling up in us. The other desires we
have held onto in our life up until then will seem less important. Then we will begin to try to figure out how we can come
into an inner spiritual life and relationship with God. We may
attend more classes, read books from many different teachings and traditions, and try out some churches and alternative
forms of spirituality. We may well gain many new insights and
inspirations from these explorations, but we may also begin
to get a sense that all the reading in the world is not going to
move us much beyond where we are in terms of actually developing something real within our beings.

This is when we may get the idea that we need help. Surely
there must be someone who can help us find our way. We may
also have read how the Eastern spiritual paths have master
teachers who train and initiate students and how those students are transformed through personal training with that

teacher and through the practices and initiations they receive. For me, the realization that I would need the help of a teacher to find my way spiritually came when I read Herman Hesse's Siddhartha when I was 16 years old.

Why do we need a spiritual teacher to grow spiritually? Why can't we just go to church, or to yoga, or to meditation classes and get into a relationship with God that way? Many people, including myself, have tried to accomplish the goal of developing a relationship with God through these means. We did gain some or perhaps even many wonderful experiences through these practices. But did we actually come into a direct and clear connection with God? Or did we still feel like God was somewhere far away and quite unknowable? I personally had serious yogic training of several kinds, followed by Sufi training, and though I had some wonderful growth through these trainings, I did not clear much of the crust off my soul and was not brought to where I could experience God directly. I wanted to be able to get my questions answered by God and receive inner guidance for my life. I was concerned that I was missing the purpose for which I had incarnated and that it would be terrible to discover that was true after I died. I realized that I needed individual training to gain those skills and clear my soul and that I would need it from someone who knew the way and could help me overcome my negative habits and remove my blockages.

How do you find a teacher once it is clear to you that you need one? There is an Eastern saying that states, "When the student is ready, the teacher will come." Your desire to begin your spiritual training will move out from you as a prayer and will begin to guide you on your journey to finding a teacher. For some people this is a very short journey; for others it takes many years. I will give you a brief description of the various kinds of spiritual teachers to help you know what you might be looking for. There are thousands of people across this country and around the world that teach classes in different spiritual disciplines such as yoga, meditation, prayer or better living through consciousness. These teachers tend to be people who have themselves found a lot of benefit from practicing the discipline they now teach and who took some, or many, courses to be able to pass their practices on to others. Most of them have good hearts and help a lot of people live with less stress and find some degree of peace and healing.

The next step up from this category of teacher is the group made up of ministers, pastors and rabbis of churches, temples and synagogues. These men and women teach and preach and try to help people get their lives in line with God's will for human beings. They teach people to be decent to other people, not to hurt others and how to find some peace in an understanding of God and of life after death. They often serve a large and good purpose all over the planet, and many people are drawn to churches, synagogues and temples of all kinds to allow these teachers and ministers to instruct them and guide them in such ways. Priests differ from ministers in that they have a greater focus on the sacraments and also act in some ways as mediators for God.

The next category of spiritual teachers contains people who have more than just theological degrees and training. They also have completed deep inner journeys and transformational work and can actually teach people how to make real connections with the spiritual world and with God. They can teach how to effectively and truly pray, how to heal yourself and others, and they can help bring spiritual light into people's beings. There are a lot fewer of these teachers, and they are also not in as much demand. Most people do not want to undertake deep, inner transformational work, but they are simply looking to ease their pain and find a bit of peace and relief from their anxiety and sadness. Such teachers can actually help a student have experiences in the spiritual world, which may help convince a person that the spiritual world is real and is worth getting to know. It is from this level up that I would say a person is a spiritual teacher, and if you are working with this kind of a teacher, you are truly on a spiritual path and are being taught. Training with such a teacher will require a significant amount of work on the part of the student and will require their willingness to make some sacrifices of things and habits to which they may be attached. If you have even a little spiritual sight, you will be able to see that such teachers carry light in their bodies and beings and have a deeper knowing of life and God. The priests in the order in which I serve are this kind of spiritual teacher and are blessings to all whom they serve.

The last category of spiritual teachers is what would be known amongst the schools of the inner path as that of master teacher, or as the Sufis would say, guide. Such teachers have gone farther in their own development than the teachers in the previous category. They have been taught and empowered by another master teacher to pass on the connection with God through direct initiation and teaching. Such a master teacher can teach you to bring light into your body and heal the darkness covering your soul. A master teacher can also remove the veil that separates your consciousness from the God-Self within you so that you can actually meet God at the center of your being, face-to-face. Such teachers are often quite difficult to find, though they are present in the inner teachings of all the major world religions. They don't tend to advertise, and not too many people understand enough about themselves as spiritual beings to know to look for such a teacher. If, however, you are one of the people who want to be able to go the entire distance on the spiritual path, you will, in fact, need to find a teacher of this caliber to bring you through those initiations and transformations.

Such teachers are most often a part of a spiritual training

school. If the school and the teacher are being effective, there will be other people whom they have trained who are now teaching at the various levels of training below that master teacher stage. Often new students will begin by being taught by lower ranking ministers. Once they move through some initiations, if they begin to go deeper themselves and have proven their dedication and commitment, the master teachers will begin to train them. In this way, the master teachers are able to work with the students who need that level of teaching, especially those who want to train to teach and minister to others. Sometimes a very new student will not want to be taught by anyone less than the master teacher. A Sufi saying states, "The smallest student needs (or thinks they need) the biggest teacher." In other words, precisely those who think they are too important to be taught by someone like a minister or priest are the ones least ready to work with a master teacher.

Some people come to spiritual centers wanting to add only a little something of truth into their lives, or they are still looking around for what might be right for them. A good spiritual school will welcome such inquiries and will be happy to share with those inquiring whatever amount of training they are interested in receiving. There is another group of people who, whether from near the beginning of finding a new path, or maybe after checking a path out for a while, say, "This is what I want. Please take me as far as I can go on this path." These people want to buckle down and do the intensive inner work. When such a person approaches me, I am happy to train them and take them as far as they choose to go. And there are people in various in-between stages.

It is up to you to decide what depth of training you want and therefore what type of school and teachers you will need. Some schools offer training on all levels and most only train on a few levels. But you may not know yet what you want because you don't know what there is to want. If that is the case,

I recommend that you check out various spiritual schools and organizations by going to introductory classes, services and events to see which one might be the best fit for you. There should not be any pressure to join anything or to keep attending when you are not ready to decide. Listen to your heart. Notice what feels right and what does not. Meditate on what you feel the God-Self wants you to do and follow that, not your thinking. Keep searching until you find what is right, but don't wait too long. Throw yourself into whatever you feel drawn to. If you need to change to another path later, you can do so. You will have benefitted from what you learned by being in that first school and you will have God's protection keeping you safe as long as your intentions are good and you listen to your heart.

May you be blessed with finding what you want for a spiritual life and developing the courage and commitment to enter into it fully, whatever form it might take.

CHAPTER FOUR

Spirit, Healing and Empowerment: How Your Spiritual Life Affects Your Ability to Heal

He complained of his pain a hundredfold.
God said, "Grief and pain make you modest and noble.
Your real enemy is your own medicine,
the elixir that seeks to win your heart.
Flee from it to solitude and seek the help of God's grace.
Your friends are really your enemies,
for they occupy you and make you oblivious of God."

~ Rumi, "Mathnawi"

A major news magazine in the United States devoted a front cover to the question of whether prayer is good medicine. Other authors and publications have addressed the combination of medicine and spiritual practices from various perspectives. Studies have shown that people who go to church or temple regularly live longer and report having happier and more fulfilled lives than those who don't. Researchers have also found that people who have other people who care about them recover faster and with greater frequency from major surgery and life-threatening illnesses. Depression has been documented to shorten lives, while feeling loved lengthens life. This is the data that keeps flowing in from the institutions studying the correlations between spiritual practices, human relationships, feelings of satisfaction with one's life, and longevity and health.

I am not a statistician, neither am I a biologist or medical sociologist, though my background has involved health care. I am a Certified Professional Midwife and practiced midwifery for seventeen years. I am also a psychotherapist with three years of post-graduate training in Jungian Psychology. I have therefore been involved in physical and mental health care.

Now my full time work is the care of souls. I counsel, teach and help guide people through their personal transformations into a life of wholeness and health. When working with people's transformations, it quickly becomes obvious that bodies, hearts, minds and souls are not separate parts of a person, unaffected by what is going on in the other parts; rather, they are all interdependent. Whatever someone carries in his mind, heart or soul will affect his physical body, and whatever is going on in the physical body can be linked to something going on in the mind, heart or soul. We are not only flesh bodies, neither are we only spirit, mind and heart. We are all of these joined together, and if you are interested in helping to heal one aspect of a person, it helps to know at least the basics of how all our parts interrelate.

As I have stated before, most of us think that we are our bodies, minds and hearts and we have souls (that is, if we believe we have souls at all). In fact, the reverse is true – we are souls, and we have bodies, minds and hearts. Why do I say this? Because how we think of this will affect the entire way we relate to our various parts. So what is a soul? A soul is the part of us that is eternal. According to mystical teachings, we have both a soul and a God-Self which are both eternal. The God-Self is at the center of our being. It is pure God and is therefore the same in everyone. The soul, on the other hand, is unique to each of us. Mystics tell that we have lived many times and that our souls have been formed by the many different experiences we have had during all our lives on earth.

We have all been male and female, rich and poor. We have had positive and negative experiences during our times in bodies. We have made good and poor choices. We have all suffered pain of heart, mind, body and soul. When we were born into this life, we already had a load of experiences, which affected us from birth. Added to those experiences from the past are our experiences from living with our families in this life. We are fortunately given a break from the burden of remembering our past lives so that we can make a fresh start in each new life on earth. But the feelings leftover from those lives and the habits and patterns we established can still come through in this life. Most of all, the conclusions we drew from our previous lives as well as those we have gathered in this life are with us and we often hold onto them as if they were self-evident truths.

The conclusions you have drawn will affect your health in many ways. Let us consider some common conclusions from past life experiences that you might have drawn and how these might be affecting your health. Imagine that in a number of past lives you have repeatedly experienced food deprivation or even starvation. Even though you always had enough food in this life, you may not truly be able to believe there is enough. You may find that you eat as though you need to store up nourishment because you feel uncertain about whether there will be food tomorrow or the next day. The consequences of such past life experiences are easy to imagine.

Another scenario might be that you were very privileged in your last life, or for several past lives. This life you may not have had everything handed to you, and you might actually need to work for a living. You find you have immense resentment for needing to work, and you feel like you are above working to make a living and are being wronged by others who hold such expectations of you. This resistance against having to work creates a string of bad employment experiences and numerous relationship problems. One solution many people with such a history discover is to become ill so that they do not need to work. The illness is then based in the basic belief that they should not have to work, making sure they are supported by others, whether by family or the government.

One more common past-life scenario: Imagine that in a past life you were terrorized and brutalized by other people. Now, in this life, even though nothing terrible has happened to you, you have all the symptoms of having had a history of immense abuse. The fear from that previous life has lodged in your soul and you believe that the world is unsafe and anything could happen to you at anytime. Your fear can become emotionally paralyzing and affect every aspect of your life and your relationships.

These same effects of past experiences can also be present when such experiences came your way in this current life. If you were deprived of food as a child, if you were treated as if you never should have to contribute anything to the world when you were growing up, or if you were abused when young, you will show the same effects as if these events occurred in a previous life. From those experiences, you will likely have drawn certain conclusions about the world and yourself as a person living in this world. These conclusions are now the underlying patterns for everything that you do in life. If you want to heal the physical, emotional, psychological and spiritual troubles that you are experiencing, you will need to first become aware of what conclusions you have drawn about the world and how those conclusions are affecting your life. Most conclusions we have we assume to be absolute truth, often without ever having checked them out with anyone else. They seem so self-evident that we believe that anyone with any intelligence would surely see things as we do. When we find that other people don't see life our way, we may conclude that they are stupid or crazy, or we may begin to question our own intelligence or sanity. If you were raised in a family that holds similar conclusions about life and the world as you do, your pattern and belief in your conclusions is deepened even more.

How then does spirituality affect people's lives and their ability to heal? In a very broad sense, we can define spirituality as how people relate to the subjects of life after death, spiritual worlds, a higher power that is above humans, and themselves as spirits rather than only bodies, minds and emotions. For some people, their spirituality consists mostly in their ponderings about the purpose of life and questions of ethics and morality. Most people's sense of spirituality also includes some belief that the power and idea behind life itself is either fundamentally loving and beneficent or hard and punishing. These beliefs become frameworks within which we try to understand all the events and experiences that we have. Our thinking and our emotions will adapt to what we believe to be true, and our bodies will eventually follow suit. Our bodies follow suit because they are directed by our minds and our emotions to be a certain way. Though our bodies have built-in patterns for health and well-being and can resist messages to the contrary for a very long time, eventually they will adopt the program that our minds and emotions dictate to them. If that program is one of disease, our bodies in time, will manifest the results and become ill.

When we look at our lives and how they have developed, we will see that we live out of our beliefs and our spirituality. When I work with my spiritual students, helping them grow into wholeness and peace, we follow the trail of sadness, anger, fear and hurt to get to the origin of those wounds in their hearts. We explore childhood and adult traumas, hurts and disappointments. And when it seems like going farther back into previous lives might shed some light on the problem and hence a better possibility for healing, I guide them through a past-life regression to see what happened to them. Over and over I find the same pattern and truth emerges. This truth is that the traumas and wounds we incur throughout our existence are not the cause of our persistent suffering and inability to heal, but rather the conclusions that we have drawn from those painful experiences are the cause of our ongoing pain and lack of well-being. Let this truth sink into you for a minute. I am saying that you are not bound by your painful past but only by what you now believe because of it.

There is good and bad news in this assertion that I am making. The good news is that although you cannot change what has already happened to you, you can in fact change the negative results you experience due to those events. By becoming conscious of conclusions you have drawn based on those events, you can decide whether you want to still hold onto those conclusions. Once you realize that your conclusions were not absolute truths about you, life, people and the world but are rather a point of view you adopted, you can then examine what other points of view people have and how those affect their lives. If you see that their beliefs about all and everything seem to allow for more peace and joy in their lives, you can consider how you can exchange your set of beliefs for a set that might give you more satisfying results.

This is where spirituality enters into a person's ability to heal and impacts their chance to feel empowered in their lives. Consider a situation in which people have been sexually abused as children by their fathers. Many people who have had this experience wrestle for the rest of their life with issues concerning sex, men, trust, authority figures, anger, resentment, and feeling disempowered. All those feelings are completely understandable and justifiable under the circumstances. Without allowing those feelings to come up and be expressed, there will be little chance of healing and moving on; however, only bringing the feelings up and expressing them will not heal the wound. Those actions will likely help ease the pain and bring some sense of empowerment, but healing still lies ahead. People who have experienced childhood sexual abuse will also need to carefully examine what conclusions they have drawn because of that experience. Do they now believe all men are bad or dangerous? Do they believe they can only be loved in a sexual way? Do they believe that all authorities are to be guarded against? Do they believe that they are damaged goods and not good enough to be with anyone who is not equally wounded? And do they believe that there is no safety or protection in the world, so they need to stay vigilant and defended at all times? Do they believe life itself is unjust, mean and hurtful, and would they rather not experience it at all?

You may be wondering how a victim of childhood abuse could not feel and believe those things. You are right – at least some of those thoughts and feelings are bound to arise, until the time when a different understanding of it all can enter in. Imagine if you have had such an experience and you have been taught that God is a male, all-powerful, and that you have no control over what God does. Would you then not be afraid of, or even hate, God? It would make sense that you would want very little to do with such a God, or that you might feel you had better be good and keep God appeased out of fear that this powerful, male father figure will hurt you beyond all imagining. Your employment and relationships would also be affected by the wound within you. Then you may ask yourself, how could spirituality be a positive force for healing?

As a mystic, what I know about God I know from my own experiences. Mystics are less interested in what others tell them about God and are more interested in finding out for themselves and by their own experiences who God is and how God functions, feels and thinks. On the mystical path, one is led into a direct relationship with God in which one can learn to feel God's presence, ask God questions and obtain answers. Through such experiences I have come to know God as the most loving, caring, compassionate and patient being one can ever imagine. A common question then is, "How could a loving God have allowed such terrible things to happen to me or to those whom I love?" This is the cry of the heart in pain.

God created souls (people) because God was so full of love that God wanted to give it away and infuse that love into others. God recognized that if God was to have a meaningful love relationship with humans, God also needed to give us the choice of not loving God. This makes sense if you consider how different love would feel if it was coming from someone who could choose to love you or not versus love coming to you from someone because they were programmed to love you. Love is not meaningful and fulfilling where there is no freedom to choose otherwise. God was so certain that God only wanted a love relationship with us when we decided to choose it that God gave us the option not to love God for however many lifetimes we wanted. And God gave us total freedom to choose to live in ways of darkness and hurt or in ways of light and love within our relationships on earth.

Try to step back and look at yourself from a many lifetimes perspective. Before you enter into each incarnation on earth you are assisted by angels and beings of light to choose where and to whom you will be born. You choose this based on what you need to learn in this life in order to move you along your path of spiritual evolution. Unfortunately, we humans learn much more deeply and clearly from our painful experiences than we do from our happy ones. Therefore, if we truly want to grow, we may courageously choose to come into a very difficult family situation, which will force us to address some issues. Each family has such challenges built into it, and each life offers us new chances to grow in our understanding and abilities to become strong, independent, speak our truth, set boundaries, forgive, heal and choose to do better than what was done to us.

Please note that just because your family and others who have hurt you allowed for you to learn and grow through the wounding does not in any way justify what they did as right. You were hurt, you were wronged, and you need to be able to feel that, acknowledge it and speak it; then comes the opportunity to grow from it. This is where your conclusions enter in. If you draw negative conclusions about people, the world, God and yourself, you will simply stay alone in your pain for your entire life. If, however, you can come to know that you are loved and are protected even though you have been hurt, you can rise up into an entirely different life. In order to do this, you will need to be able to experience God's love. Through coming to know God yourself, you can begin to make sense of why you might have chosen your family and why God allowed bad things to happen to you. You will not be able to feel good about life, yourself and others if you hold onto a belief that God is bad or is at least a failure for not having come through in protecting you.

Knowing that God is a loving being, not a mean or uncaring one, will open the way for you to see the meaning and opportunity in everything in your life. So what is to be gained from having been abused as a child? Imagine that in your past lives you repeatedly stayed under your parents' control, never breaking free to be yourself. You allowed them to hold power over you and determine how you lived. If that was your history, and you were seeing the necessity to break that pattern so you could live your own life, might you not choose to have parents that hurt you so badly that by necessity you gather enough strength to say, "No more!" and move away from them? When I take people back to other lives, I often see just this. I see that they were stuck in a pattern for a long time and decided to up the ante this time and enter into a situation that was so intolerable that they would have to change it. Sometimes we may instead be experiencing what it is like to be the recipient of some negative actions we were doing to others in previous lives. What better way to learn not to inflict abuse on others than to be on the receiving end and feel the extent of the damage done through abuse, and thereby never choose to do that to another person again. If I had been hurting people in a particular way over several lifetimes, I would want to be the recipient of that hurt to cut that pattern out of me so that I never do it again. So either way, whether the reason for entering into a painful family is to learn to break loose of some abuse we ourselves perpetuated against others, or to learn through immense pain to gather up the strength to become stronger, both will have been worth it, don't you think?

I know this can be hard to hear and accept when you have been so hurt and so angry for a very long time. But do you see how I am presenting you with a road to freedom from your anger and pain? I am also aware that you may not feel ready to be free of those feelings. You certainly have the right to choose when and if you want to let those feelings go and head into healing. You don't have to ever let them go if you don't choose to. You can carry them throughout this life and into the next one. You will know when you are ready. And when you are, know that there are those who can help you to heal from your past and enter into a whole new understanding about life, about God and creation, about people, about love, and about yourself. When, in fact, you open to the truth that the power that guides the universe and your life is entirely loving, then you can begin to understand your life in such a way that initiates the healing. You can then, with the help of someone who holds the bigger picture, come to know yourself as someone who does have power to choose, who has always been loved by God, who has everything needed to become entirely whole.

May these truths nourish the growth of hope in your heart,

and if you are in a helping profession, may you bring that hope to others. We who help others must first be helped. Often the ones who feel a desire to help others want to skip over the step of getting help for themselves first. I encourage those of you who want to bring others into greater health and peace to treat yourselves to your own healing. Allow yourself to be guided so that you can find where the conclusions you drew from your wounds keep life from flowing through you as abundantly as it could. Find the way that works best for you to draw close and come to God as the profoundly loving presence that God is. Once you allow God to do so, God will change your life into a flowing fountain of peace and well-being for all those around you. May you be blessed as you find your way into being healed and allowing yourself to be filled with peace.

CHAPTER FIVE

Between a Rock and a Hard Place: Fitting a Spiritual Life into an Already Busy Schedule

God is of no importance unless He is of supreme importance.

~ Rabbi Abraham Joshua Heschel, "Man is Not Alone"

Since you are reading this book, you are likely a person who feels the need or has the longing to have the spiritual be part of your life. You had to make an effort, maybe even a considerable one, to obtain this book and make the time to read it. But you did make that effort, because somehow finding a way to have a meaningful spiritual life has become important to you. This desire for the spiritual may be a new feeling for you, and you may want to explore the options. Or you may have been feeling this desire for quite a while, but have not until now found or made the time for this exploration. You may have alternatively been checking out various churches, spiritual schools or teachings. Whichever of these may describe what brought you to this point of delving into these studies of true mysticism and profound truths, I welcome you upon this way. If you open your heart and still your mind you will, through these readings, begin to have a sense of what the spiritual path really is and how you can make space for it in your life.

When people begin to feel the urge, the need and the longing to have a spiritual life, a very specific thing happens inside of their beings. When you recall that each of us is a soul and has a body, mind and feelings, you will begin to see many things differently. You will then understand why, sooner or later, whether this lifetime or another, we will all long to have a spiritual life. I am defining the word "soul" as that which we are in our essence, which travels from one life to another. Our souls have been formed and developed through all the experiences we have ever had throughout the many lives we have lived, while holding at the center of our souls, the God-Self, that spark in each of us which is pure God. It is often referred to as God within.

When you begin to long for a spiritual life or you really feel a need for it, it is actually your soul that is sounding the call to your heart and mind. It is saying that it is time for you to begin your journey toward becoming who you really are, in your essence, and toward coming into a close and clear relationship with God within you. The importance of this call arising from our souls cannot be overstated. From the point of view of the eternal part of you, nothing in all of life matters more than the undertaking of this journey. Your career does not matter to your soul, except in how it allows your soul to grow and express in certain ways, and your relationships have a similar value to your soul. Insofar as your work or career and the significant relationships in your life develop you as a being and allow you to learn love, selflessness, patience, discipline, tolerance and other positive qualities, then from the soul's point of view, they are useful. If, however, they become the central focus and the be-all and end-all of your life, they will instead get in the way of your soul's purpose and development.

Most people allow their work, their relationships and sometimes their hobbies or other interests to become the central focus of their lives. Our society condones this. People who love their partner, their children and their work above all are considered to be the best of people, especially those who love their partner and children more than anything else. Whatever happened to the great commandment that states, "You shall love your God with all your heart, and all your soul, and with all your mind. And you shall have no other gods before the One God." How many of our love songs have phrases such as, "You are everything I am living for; nothing matters more to me than you; I adore you, live only for you, care about nothing but you." We tend to get all mushy about such wonderful love. How many times do you hear about people who gave up everything for their children? How many women, especially, truly believe that that is what they are supposed to be doing if they are in order to be good mothers?

This may sound shocking to you, but I am telling you that that is, in fact, a life and a value system that is out of balance. I am not saying that our committed relationships, our deep love for our partner and our immense love for our children are bad. They most certainly are not bad. They fulfill us and teach us and stretch us and sweeten our lives in so many ways. People without such relationships are often missing out on some of the best experiences that life has to offer. The problem arises when these relationships take the central place in our lives. When that happens, we have lost touch with our soul and with our soul's purpose for being in a body and living on earth.

You may be even more shocked by this next statement: All the good that a person may do, all one's charitable work, all the helpfulness one may give should not take the place of making a direct connection with God. Mother Theresa of Calcutta, who is so honored and revered for all the good works she did for the poor, once said that what really matters is our prayers. She said that you can't pray all the time and you have to do some-thing between prayer-times, so do something useful! And look at all the useful things she managed to do between doing what mattered most to her – communing with God.

Here is the key to having a meaningful, deep, spiritual life while living a full life in the world. We must start by placing God and our work to come into relationship with God at the very center of our lives. We must decide to have no other gods before God. That means that our partner, our children, our work and all other activities and relationships must take second place to our quest to come into a deep and direct experience of God. When you do this, an amazing thing will happen; suddenly you will find you do have time to pursue the spiritual path. When you get your priorities straight, you will find your spiritual teacher and discover that you can fit the inner work and the work you will do with your spiritual community into your life without a problem.

Does this mean that we should neglect our children, our partner, our work and other obligations? Absolutely not. Instead, we will, through our spiritual work, learn how to become more efficient, more loving, more patient and more caring. All those around us will benefit from the new light, life and love we bring with us into all our relationships. We will uplift and bless our loved ones with the spiritual energy we will come to carry. But we first have to take that crucial step of making our spiritual lives come before all else in our lives.

Placing God and the goal of coming to know God face-to-face at the very center of your life is the one and only way to walk the spiritual path seriously and with deep, lasting results. God cannot be an afterthought to the rest of your life. You will never be able to fit God into the periphery of your life. If you try to do that, you will find that it doesn't work. You will never find enough time to meditate, pray or work with a spiritual teacher. Your growth will be slow and frustrating, leaving you always feeling like you should be able to do more, experience more and grow more. You will see others around you growing much faster and wonder why that is not happening for you.

For many people, a nagging guilt and other bad feelings continue to surface in them about not really having made a connection with God. These feelings do not let up until they make that connection and come into a real relationship with God.

When God and your relationship with God take center stage in your life and you begin to work with a teacher, you will be amazed at how fast you start having spiritual experiences and how you will grow and transform. In the school where I teach, every student gets individual instruction and guidance from a priest or teacher on a bi-weekly basis. Everyone is given spiritual exercises and studies to do which are right for them and which will launch their spiritual life into high gear. This is the kind of instruction you will need to find if you really want to move into the deeper spiritual realities. Reading books and working on your own or with a group of peers can only take you so far but those will not take you into the deeper spiritual realities. .

The spiritual path is not vague or unclear as to where it leads. It may seem so to those who have not walked it. Real spiritual teachers of any of the great world religions' inner paths (whether they be Sufi, Buddhist, Shaman, or mystical Jewish or Christian) will all teach the same path. They will teach it different ways, and some of those paths are significantly faster than others. But the steps will be the same because all of them will lead you from where you are now, through working with the light and receiving initiations, which bring the light into your body, to where you come into a face-to-face relationship with God within you. Nothing in your life could be more important. Nothing will bring more joy and peace and depth to your everyday. It all begins with giving God back God's rightful place at the center of your life.

As I said earlier, the soul is the one that calls out to your heart and mind, filling you with a desire to have a meaningful spiritual life. That you are reading this now is an indicator that your soul may already be calling to you in this way and that you are hearing it. Until a person's soul calls out, that person will have no interest in that which is spiritual. If you mention something spiritual to a person whose soul has not called out to him, he will likely stare at you blankly, or he will misunderstand and interpret what you said as being something different. But once your soul calls you, it will take considerable effort on your part to shut it up. You can shut it up if you try hard, but the longing to become whole and to have a deep relationship with God will leave an empty feeling in you if you do not find a way to respond to it.

Once you do decide to make this the most important thing in your life, as I stated before, you will need to find someone to teach you. The mystical path, which is the path we work with and teach, is one in which each individual comes into his or her own experiences rather than accepting someone else's teachings about God. Anyone embarking on this path and wanting to go far will absolutely need a teacher. The universe set it up this way to make sure that only those who are humble enough to ask someone to teach them and who will follow direction will rise up to teach others. It works very well to weed out the proud and arrogant early on the path. For one cannot seek to know God without becoming humble and becoming willing to be led.

I want this to be clear and simple for you, so that you know what you will need to do if you want to follow your soul's urgings: 1) You need to make your spiritual life the top priority in your life around which you build everything else. 2) You need to find someone to teach you and begin studying with him or her. If you have found a good teacher, from there on all will be guided, and you will come to achieve your goal according to how much you are willing to be transformed by the new truths and experiences of the divine that you will have. Being between a rock and a hard place refers to being between the rock, which is a symbol of the God-Self at the center of your being, and the hard place, which is the world in which we live. You will have to navigate that journey from the hard place to the rock, from the outer world to the inner. There your soul will be filled. There it will find peace. There you will become who you truly are and will be able to fulfill your mission on earth.

Mystical Roses of Peace

CHAPTER SIX

Death and Resurrection

*It is often thought that the Buddha's doctrine teaches us that
suffering will disappear if one has meditated long enough,
or if one sees everything differently. It is not that at all.
Suffering isn't going to go away;
the one who suffers is going to go away.*

~ Ayya Khema, "When the Iron Eagle Flies"

The concepts of death and resurrection are ones most of us
have grown up with since we live in a predominately Christian
culture. Most Americans would associate these terms with
the life of Jesus Christ but would be hard-pressed to come up
with how these terms fit into their experience of life, except
perhaps as the hope for life after death. There is, however, an
important place that death and resurrection hold in the lives
of those who choose to pursue the inner path, the path of the
mystic. Mystics do not settle for believing or not believing any
dogmas, but instead follow a path that leads to first-hand experiences of the unseen world and of those beings who live
there. They have courageously delved into their own inner beings to the point where they could be brought, through the initiation of self-realization, into a direct, face-to-face experience
of God at their center.

The mystical approach to the lives of Jesus Christ and Mary, his mother, is to see every action they took and every event in their lives as symbolic steps along the inner path of spiritual development. By understanding the meaning of each event in their lives, we obtain a road map for our own development toward becoming whole, which is the aim of the spiritual path. Jesus' death and resurrection are absolutely key to what his service was to humankind and led to his receiving titles such as "Lord of Earth" and "King of Kings." We can therefore deduce that these events will also play important parts in the lives of those of us who seek to come into inner union with God. So what do death and resurrection mean for us today, and how can we come to enter into what they have to offer?

Any person who is conscious of wanting to grow and develop during this lifetime will come across difficult times when they have to face their shortcomings. This often happens when, during painful situations, we discover parts of ourselves and how we act that we do not like at all. We can at such times dig in our heels and persist in these habitual ways of being, defending them as "just how we are," or we can decide to change. If we do, in fact, decide to change, then we will first need to thoroughly understand ourselves, what that pattern of behavior is and why we do it. Only then will we be able to decide to act otherwise and go about changing the pattern in our thinking, feelings and actions. The process of stopping how we used to act, react, think and feel, and of consciously setting about changing is a process of dying to who we were and then resurrecting to a new, consciously chosen way of being in this world. There will be a sense of loss of the old you, some grieving of it and sometimes a difficult time between that death and what is to emerge. But when the new way of being in this world comes, it is much like the freshness of spring and new life. It brings with it all the miraculous energies of resurrection and of life emerging out of death.

We who teach this mystical Christian path absolutely and un-equivocally attest to the fact that complete transformation of a person is possible. As students work with us, we see without a doubt – and they experience – major changes taking place in them. The object of the inner path is not to become some prescribed image of someone else who is more holy. The object is to become more and more yourself and to be free of the negative thinking and feelings that have kept you from becoming yourself before. We work with our students to help them see how they have perpetuated the situations that make them miserable and how beautiful they truly are when those negative conditions are not ruling their lives. We call forth their greatest potential and help them overcome that which has held them back up until now. We do all this so that they may come to know the God at the center of their beings and thereby also come to know why they are on earth and what they are to contribute to this planet during this lifetime. We are all here with individual purposes and it is a great tragedy for us not to come to know what our purpose on earth is and how we can fulfill it.

One of the greatest fears people tend to have about entering into training with a spiritual teacher is that they will be ex-pected to become someone else – like the ideal example that school portrays a spiritual person to be. They are afraid they will need to talk and dress a certain way, eat, sleep and act as the other members of that group do. They are afraid they will have to lose what they consider to be essentially themselves and to become someone else whom they may not recognize or like. Everyone has heard of religious groups that have such re-quirements. A true spiritual school or training program would never seek to have people all become the same. Quite the con-trary, we seek to have emerge out of each student that which is so uniquely them that there is none other like it on the planet. We celebrate the diversity of expression and delight in seeing such diversity in our students.

I have stated that the God-Self at the center of each person is identical, but because no two people have had the same life experiences, especially not over many lives, each soul is unique. The God-Self at the center of each soul gives off light, which then shines through the soul. That light will shine differently through each person because of the variations of their souls; hence, there are a variety of expressions of people once they have stripped away all the outer societal conditioning which told them how they should express and be in the world. The soul cannot shine through very well until that outer conditioning has been cleared away.

The God-Self at the center of your being is meant to be running your life. It is in contact with all the knowledge on earth and in the spiritual world and therefore knows exactly what you need and how you can best enjoy life while contributing to the evolution of this planet. It is, however, clouded over until we decide that we do want contact with it and we do want to let it direct our lives. Until we make that decision, we allow our conscious minds to direct our lives. Your conscious mind does not have access to wisdom or the bigger picture of you and your life; it has been formed mostly by your environment, and it cannot judge what is best other than by its own limited experience and what it hears from the world around it. It can, at times, get signals from your feelings and from your intuition, which are closer to the God-Self within. When it listens to feelings and intuition, it can make better decisions than when it only has thought to work with, but those faculties are still limited in scope.

The aim of the inner mystical spiritual path, no matter whether it is the Buddhist, Sufi, Native American, Kabalistic or Christian, is to get us where we can come into contact with that great inner Self and can then allow it to begin to talk with us and tell us how we actually fit into the big picture of all and everything. Ancient cultures would often take people through initiations in which they simulated dying and coming back to life. These were considered the most advanced and powerful initiations. In our mystical school, we work with these forces within the psyche of each person. We also have initiations that are offered to people once they have developed to where they can work with them and when they are ready for the transformational power that will come to them through the initiation. Every initiation involves dying to what you previously knew and worked with and being reborn into a deeper, fuller understanding and connection to God within you.

A person who seriously wants to walk the spiritual path needs to care more about making that connection with the God-Self, and thereby universal wisdom and supreme love, than they care about staying the same. You cannot simultaneously have a new connection, development and understanding and still remain unchanged. Many people find that they are deeply attached to staying exactly as they are, even though how they are actually makes them feel quite unhappy and stuck. The spiritual path is therefore for courageous people who are willing to experience the death of those parts of their lives which are no longer helpful to their growth and do not bring joy to themselves or to others. Those are the people who will experience the miracle of resurrecting to a life suffused with peace and the loving, guiding presence of the God spirit within them.

I am deeply dedicated to putting myself out of a job by connecting people so thoroughly to God within that they can get all the instruction and help that they need from within themselves and will no longer need anyone to teach and guide them. When people reach that point, they can move in freedom and peace through the world and through their lives and will be a blessing to all those with whom they come in contact. They will have access to all the wisdom of the cosmos, will be able to bring into their lives what they need and will be able to share that with others around them. But do remember the following: The way to that state of being is through dying to a life in which the conscious mind and the ego rule and resurrecting to a life in which God is at the center. This is a real inner death, and a person's longing for such a connection with God and such a life of peace and service must be very strong to want to go through this death. Once one has tasted such a life of connection, the delight of it makes it much easier to go on.

There are numerous esoteric and mystical schools around the world. However, many of them are lacking the means to bring their students through to this new life. They have many good teachings, often not so different from what I teach. But they rarely have teachers and priests who have been trained and initiated into bringing others into the experience of direct contact with the inner God. Receiving the sacraments is also a great help to spiritual students who are seeking to move along the path to the God-Self. In addition, students benefit from ongoing classes, which help them to understand and progress along this way. Without one-on-one guidance and instruction, most students will find that it is nearly impossible to move into a deep and powerful knowing of God. Each of our blind spots is just that – we can't see what we can't see and that area is precisely the one that is most likely obstructing your way to God within.

Ask yourself this question: Do you have the kind of relationship with God, either within or outside of yourself, which you would like to have? Do you feel hungry for more connection with the spiritual world? If you wonder what you are on this planet for and wish you had a way of knowing how you can help make it a better place for all the life on and in it; if you were to be told you were dying soon and wouldn't feel very comfortable with how you have lived this life and what you know about life after death; if you don't feel ready to enter what some might call the heaven world or the spiritual world; if you wish you knew how to prepare for your life after you leave your body – know that there is help for all those questions and concerns. It is up to you to take the steps to begin to have all your questions answered and all your concerns met.

It is your birthright as a human being to experience the fullness of the divine presence within you and, in that connectedness, to be able to have all of your needs met and more. Jesus said, "It is God's good pleasure to give you the kingdom," meaning God wants you to have everything you want and need, in abundance. You just have to know how to make the connection and how to ask. Jesus said, "Ask, and it will be given to you; seek and you shall find; knock and it will be opened to you." How to ask, how to seek and how to knock is all you need to know; and all you need to have is fuel for the journey – the burning desire to come into that knowing. May the desire of your heart be given to you.

Mystical Roses of Peace

CHAPTER SEVEN

The Ties that Bind Us to the Past

I will persist until I succeed. Always will I take another step.
If that is of no avail, I will take another, and yet another.
In truth, one step at a time is not too difficult...
I know that small attempts, repeated,
will complete any undertaking.

~ Og Mandino

What is it that keeps us tied to the past? What makes us do the same patterns of behavior or re-experience the same situations and issues over and over? Why can't we just let go of what happened to us long ago, or how things once were, and be here now? The Book of Isaiah in the Old Testament says, "The spirit of the Lord is upon me; because the Lord has anointed me to preach the good tidings unto the meek; he has sent me to heal the brokenhearted, to proclaim liberty to the captives, and the opening of prison to them that are bound." Jesus began his ministry by reading this scripture in the temple, and then proclaiming that he was the one who was spoken of in that passage and that it was he who would bring us those bless-ings. Those of us who serve the light have the same mission. We have been anointed to preach good tidings to the meek, to heal the brokenhearted, to proclaim liberty to the captives, and to open the prison to those who are bound. Using this scripture and the actions described in it, I will attempt to make clear to you what the ties are that bind you to the past. I want to let you know that there can be healing for your broken hearts, liberty for you who are captive; those prisons that still hold you can be opened.

This scripture actually holds the whole truth about what the work is that some of us have taken on and how we help those (who want us to) to be free of the ties that bind them to the past. There are four actions in the scripture: Preaching the good tidings to the meek; healing the broken hearted; proclaiming liberty to the captives; and opening the prison for those that are bound. Notice that the first and the third things are about teaching and preaching: Preaching good tidings to the meek and proclaiming liberty to captives. The second and fourth are about actions: Healing the brokenhearted and opening the prison for those who are bound. As spiritual teachers of the Christian mysteries we first teach you and joyfully let you know that, if you are meek, you can be free of the past. Then we help you heal your broken heart. Once you have healed at least somewhat, we teach you again: We let you know that you can be totally free of all that binds you. Then, when you are ready, we open your prison doors so you can walk into that total freedom. How do we of the Christian mystical path do all that with our students? What are the steps you could be making and preparing to become free of the ties that bind you?

I will begin with the first action we take in our mission to set people free: We preach good tidings to the meek. Who are the meek? Are you meek? The meek are those who do not resist the truth and the influx of God into their bodies, minds, hearts, and souls. Mother Mary is our supreme example of meekness. She was so meek that she could receive the spirit of God into her body and allow it to inseminate her, and she could hold the Christ in a physical form within her and grow it to maturity.

She was meek enough to not consider herself too good, or not good enough, for the task; she simply asked that it be done unto her according to God's will. She was so meek that she accepted titles such as "Mother of God" and "Queen of Heaven" when she was asked to do so. Therefore, to those of you who are meek, who are willing to receive the good news, I say: You can be transformed, you can come to know God face-to-face, and you can come to be of service to God and be a part of God's plan for the transformation of the earth. These are the good tidings we have for you, and to the degree that you are meek and do not resist, each of them will become a reality in your life.

Why would anyone want to resist that good news? Why would you want to resist the news that you can be transformed, that you can know God, and that you can serve in the transformation of the Earth? This is important for you to consider because the whole rest of the process is dependent upon your having no resistance to this truth. Let's look at the possible reasons for a person's resistance to this news. What could be your resistance to hearing that you can be transformed? You need to deeply meditate on whether you actually want to be transformed and what you understand transformation to mean.

If you are like most people, you probably would be very glad to have those parts of you transformed that are an embarrassment to you. Everybody has times when they regret ways they acted or reacted, when they displayed insecurities or fears that made them look weak in their own eyes or the eyes of others. Wouldn't it be nice to have those things in you changed, to never again face those embarrassing moments! I would also venture to say that everyone would be glad to have their sadness and anxieties transformed into bliss and eternal peace. We would like to be smarter, better looking, wittier, strong, loving, supportive, responsive, brilliant, devoted, committed, responsible and productive. So, why might we resist transformation? And which aspects in us would we resist having transformed? The aspects of yourself that you most likely do not want to have transformed are the ones which you either believe are essential to your survival or which you are proud and believe to be "right." God allows everyone to take as long as they want to face these things and decide they want to transform them. Real spiritual teachers do the same. We will honor your choice to retain those patterns in your life until you are ready to shed them.

The second piece of good news is that you can meet God face-to-face. Why might you resist that? Isn't it what you long and hope for? In fact, when students begin to be guided in the direction of the God-Self within many resistances come up. Most people dream of having themselves quite perfected, and in that perfected form they want to meet God, so that God will not be able to find fault in them. Rarely does someone want to have the perfection of God pouring down upon them and illuminating every nook and cranny of their beings when they do not feel like they have been totally transformed. Once again, meekness comes up. Are you meek enough to accept God fully into your being, without wanting to withhold all those parts that are embarrassingly imperfect? Have you got enough humility to stand, as you are, in that light and accept God's love for you in the shape you are in?

You see, it is not your job to get perfect before you meet God. If that were the case, you would never be able to meet God. Your job, instead, is to open all of yourself to God to be transformed, without any concepts or opinions about how God is to do that. Then as God shows you how God wants you to address those things, you do the work necessary, in humility and love. How do you open like that? You do it first of all by opening to a spiritual teacher in that same way just described. The more open you learn to be with a teacher and the less you try to hide things that are embarrassing and that you feel ashamed of from yourself and them, the more easily you will be able to do so with God. You will find when you open to a teacher that they don't really care what you have in your past, on your conscience, or in the present, as long as you are willing to expose it and have it forgiven and transformed. God will respond the same way to your embarrassing and shameful stuff. Once you give up your ideas of how perfect you should be before you meet God and your ideas of how to go about becoming that way, then you will be able to fully open to God and receive the influx of God's love into your body, mind, heart and soul.

The third piece of good news is that you can come to be of service to God and be a part of God's plan for the transformation of the planet. Why might anyone want to resist that? Or maybe you are asking, why would anyone not want to resist that? What does it mean, anyhow? Through Jesus' teachings in the New Testament, it is clear that there will be a change of consciousness on this planet. This past century has shown more changes than all of the previous centuries combined. In this accelerated pace of change, the spiritual aspect of human consciousness has not kept up. Most people are no clearer about what God is and how to connect with God than people were two thousand years ago. God's plan for the planet is for everyone to be able to carry the light in their bodies and have a direct relationship with God. When that occurs, there will be no need for wars and famines, poverty and hatred. There will be no need for addictions, depressions, anxieties, and all other forms of mental and emotional illness. Then, indeed, the lion will lay down with the lamb, and there will be peace on Earth.

In order for that to come about, increasing numbers of people need to be carrying that light and bringing it to others. Each of us can be of use in that plan. Why might we not want to? Usually, it is because we think we have a better plan for our lives. We think our professions, our families, or our hobbies and interests all matter more. I believe that at the end of your life, you would like to feel that you were leaving the planet a better place for having been here. Can you then imagine anything more important than bringing more of the light into the consciousness of the earth by taking it on yourself and helping others to take it on? Could anything matter more, not only to any kids you may have, but also to all future generations? The quality of the world your descendants will live in will likely be more affected by this work than by any other work you can do! You can, of course, also do other meaningful work, in a job or at home with kids and family. But you have to expand your consciousness to take in the enormity of the planetary work that is needed and your unique opportunity to participate in it.

Most of you might resist being a part of the transformation of the planet because you are too tied to your small worlds and have trouble thinking beyond the care of your families, jobs, and their small concerns. I am, of course, not advocating that you do not take care of your kids, marriage, and career. I am suggesting that you put them in the right priority in your life, and thereby you would not be kept from the joy of being able to be a part of the great cosmic work into which you are being invited.

Once we have taught you at least the basics of what the good news is and have helped you to begin to drop some of your resistance to it, the second thing that we as spiritual teachers do is help bring about the healing of your broken heart. Our hearts get broken as small children when our parents are not what we need them to be or what we hoped they would be. They may have abused us, or other people around us may have, or they may have neglected to give us the love, attention, support, and validation we felt we needed. And later, when grown, almost all humans will get their hearts broken through romantic love. Even if you never have an experience of loving someone and being rejected, you will still, even in the best of marriages, come up against the feeling that this was not all that you had hoped for. Something is lacking, and if you allow that feeling to flare up, you will feel how it breaks your heart. We can have our hearts broken by our peers, as kids or as adults, by friends, by mentors, teachers, counselors, ministers, or priests.

When our hearts break we develop scar tissue over those hurt places in our hearts. Scar tissue is rigid and lifeless. We also develop a great fear of a similar thing happening to us again. We decide that it is not safe to trust anyone who might inflict such pain on us, and we build huge defenses to protect ourselves. We also develop an elaborate alarm system within ourselves that is set off anytime anything remotely similar to the original assault appears upon our radar screens. What has this all got to do with spiritual development? When your spiritual teacher responds to your request to teach you and help you move along the spiritual path and begins to help you bring the light closer to you and to take it into your being, your teacher will run into those hurt places and those scars. When I work with students, I find great big barricades over those hurts, which clearly say, "Do not enter here!" Since I honor your right to keep me out from any place you don't want me to go, I will not push any further, as God also does not. When I come across one of those places in you that has been very hurt, you may feel threatened and afraid that I will hurt you also; that is why your defenses go up.

Herein lies the problem: The only way those places in you can get healed is for you to open them up to the daylight. Just as any other wound needs air to heal, so do these. When you keep them hidden inside, they can stay open wounds and fester for your whole life. The way to air them out is first to tell your teacher about them. Once you have opened up your pain and shame and guilt to them, they can begin to help you bring healing to these places. In our spiritual school, we do that through memory healings, through other guided visualizations, and sometimes through past-life regressions and other means. Our aim is to gently help you find out that you can trust Jesus and Mary with these wounds and that the light will help them heal, not make the hurt deeper. But without you first telling your teacher about the wounds, he or she is not permitted, by cosmic law, to push farther than you invite him or her to come into your psyche. So it is essential that you not withhold those stories of your past from your teacher. That is the first step toward healing your broken heart. Without healing your heart, you will only be able to function "half-heartedly," and you will only be able to receive all the great experiences of the path in part – namely, in the part that you have brought to the light. So we ask you to trust us, which we know is a very big request on our part. But we do so because there is no other way for us to help you heal. We will understand how badly it hurts; we will have empathy for your pain and sorrow, shame and guilt. And then we will take you to Jesus and Mary to be healed.

Once again, you will need to be meek, meaning you will need to not resist the healing process. Why would anyone resist healing a broken heart? Many people resist this because they come to identify themselves by their wounds. You might find it quite frightening to imagine yourself without your wounds. You might worry that you would not know who you are and could lose your identity if you were no longer wounded. We wish you to know the truth instead: You will not lose who you are; you will only lose your pain. You will, instead, for the first time, be able to be who you really are, instead of a bundle of wounds. You will feel better than you have ever felt before. But obtaining that healing hinges on whether you will let the great physicians, Jesus and Mary, and your teachers, as their servants, near enough to examine your wounds and to prescribe the right medicine for your healing. So we ask you to open up to us, honestly, deeply, and completely so that we may bring the healing light into all those places that hurt and then bring you peace and joy.

Let me now proclaim liberty to you, the captives. This is the proclamation: You really can become free of all that binds you. Likely you can't even imagine what that would look and feel like. I can see that possibility in every one, and I see the beauty and power that will be you when you take hold of that freedom. It is yours for the taking if you are willing to do the work to get there. What is that work? That work is what a real spiritual teacher does with you, and what God does with you. It is the last of the parts of the scripture we are following now. It is when God and we, working with God, open the prisons to those who are bound.

This last description of the work we do relates to a more advanced place on the spiritual path. It has to do with your crucifixion: Your complete dying unto yourself, so that you may rise again in Christ Sophia. This most often comes to a person around the time of being ordained a priest, or the equivalent of that ordination in a different school. When I tell a student who is a practicing deacon that they may begin training for the priesthood if they so choose, it is because God has shown me that that person has done enough of the inner work and has demonstrated adequate potential and preparation to enter into the process of the crucifixion. I know this is way beyond where most people are. But I want you to have some understanding of what the inner process of becoming a priest or its equivalent is and what lies ahead for any of you who are called and who choose to do the work to become such a servant of the Most High.

Take a moment; close your eyes and visualize the following: See yourself as you would be if you were not a captive to your ties to people in your life. What would that feel like in your body, your heart and your mind? Bask in that a moment to get a real feeling for it. Now visualize and feel in your body what you would feel like if you were not captive to the material things that you are so attached to. Get a real sense of being free from those feelings of attachment to your possessions. And, lastly, visualize and experience what it would be like to not be a captive to your attitudes and your fears. Go through each – one by one – and feel what you would be like, see what you would be like, if you were not caught up in these attitudes, these fears.

Did you get a sense of what you could be like, what your life might feel like, if you were not tied to those things in your life, world, mind and heart? When you begin to walk down the path of crucifixion, the cutting of ties has to go even much deeper than that. Now you truly prepare to leave the world behind within your own consciousness and your own being. And the way to being able to leave it behind is to dig ever deeper into every aspect of your fears, your shame and your pride, your beliefs and your attachments. When I work with someone during this process, I hone in on every place a person wants to hide and preserve him or herself. I leave no stone unturned to find what people are holding onto that is keeping them from giving themselves completely in service to God. I find every prison cell in them that is locked by shame or pride, attachment or fear and open that prison cell to let those feelings that are bound up inside them be set free. God wants to express and love through every part of a priest. Every locked cell is an avenue that God cannot move through that priest and can therefore not bless people through them.

As a priest in training moves through this process, they will feel squeezed and shown up at every turn. In the Bible, Jesus likens it to being as grapes put through a winepress or to grapevines being pruned so they can bear more fruit. The level of painfulness in this process is directly proportionate to the level of resistance to giving everything up. What exactly does one have to give up on this part of the path? Some of the big things are that you give up your right to defend yourself and you give up your right to an opinion. That does not mean that you become a puppet, but rather that you let us take you into every nook and cranny of your mind and heart and allow us to show you everything that is in the way of God's love moving though you. So you are giving up the right to defend yourself against us taking you into a particular place in you or maintaining the right to control the process yourself. Think about that; mull it over. I want you to feel how big that is so that you can feel the respect and awe due to the priests who have allowed themselves to be put through this. The pressure does not let up with the priest ordination either, but it keeps right up afterwards as they continue in that process of opening completely and letting go of everything in them that God cannot flow through.

This is not something one is ready for at an early stage on the spiritual path. It is rather something that one can grow towards and gets prepared for through all the previous stages of growth and letting go. In the process of the path, one needs to have developed a very deep trust in God and in one's teachers. One needs to have come to a place where one wants nothing more than to serve God and is willing to do whatever it takes to do that. At that point, one could dance and sing with the Sufi mystic Rumi, saying: "I want burning, burning, burning!" and would know what joy and ecstasy await those who allow everything to be purged out of them, leaving only pure and holy love. Those then become the highly blessed souls who are allowed to serve at God's altar and give everything through love to their fellow humans. Those are the ones who, as the scripture reads, are anointed to preach the good news, to heal the brokenhearted, to proclaim liberty to the captives, and open the prisons to those who are bound. Through the vows they make when being ordained as priests they have made eternal ties to God, Jesus and Mary and have loosed all ties to the earth. That is why the angels weep for joy for every person who takes up the cross and follows Jesus into the priesthood of love.

I invite you therefore to allow your teachers to preach the good news to you, to heal your broken hearts, to proclaim liberty to you in your captivity, and, if you are called to the priesthood and want to serve that way, that you allow them to open all the prison cells in you and set you free. May God bless you in your process of becoming free.

CHAPTER EIGHT

The Ties that Bind Us to the Future

*A vow is a purely religious act that cannot be taken
in a fit of passion. It can be taken only with
a mind purified and composed and with God as witness.*

~ Mohandas Gandhi

You now know about the ties that bind us to our past, our problems and the patterns we get stuck in. There is also a great power inherent in our ability to consciously create ties that bind us toward the purpose of our growth and service. In Matthew 16: 18-19, Jesus is quoted as saying to the Apostle Peter, "And I say to you that you are Peter, and upon this rock I will build my church; and the gates of hell will not prevail against it. And I will give you the keys of the kingdom of heaven: and whatsoever you bind on earth shall be bound in heaven: and whatsoever you loose in earth shall be loosed in heaven."

Jesus gave to the Apostle Peter, as the head of the church, the power to bind and unbind through the use of his word. That power is also given to every priest. The Apostle Peter was made head of the church – not the Roman Church as it imagines – but of the true church. The true church is the assembly of those upon the inner path and the church of the real priesthood, which is based on spiritual attainment, not on educational degrees. The authority within that church has been handed down from teacher to student ever since Jesus handed it to the Apostle Peter. That is the true Apostolic Succession, not the one the Roman Catholic Church claims to have.

Jesus gave Peter and all true priests the power to attach things to our souls and the power to cut them loose from our souls. This means that a priest can, in fact, by that power, grant a person absolution from their sins. Priests can cut the ties between people when that relationship needs to end. In the same way, priests can establish a tie between people and things, which is binding upon their souls. An example of that is the mystical marriage blessing we use in the Order of Christ Sophia. In it, the priest can actually tie those two souls together by his or her word. Priests can also hold a person accountable for something they did or failed to do. The priest's word upon it will be respected in heaven and in earth, and the person will not be able to get around it, no matter what.

That same power of tying and loosing bonds that is given to priests, from the Apostle Peter on down, is available to everyone, in a lesser degree. This means that you have the God-given ability and right to attach yourself to whatever you choose. In the same way, you can detach yourself from whatever you choose. This is a great gift and power that all people can use, although very few are even aware of having it. The form that is probably most familiar to people is that of taking a vow. Many people will acknowledge that when one takes a vow, something happens. It is more than only saying that we intend on doing something or that this is our plan. When we take a vow it is understood that we are appealing to a much higher power to take us by our word and to make that word hold. It involves the soul. People who know we have souls know that to be true, no matter what religion they belong to. They know that when we make a vow, God is involved, and we stand as souls before God for either the fulfilling or breaking of that vow.

In Numbers 30: 2 it is written, "If a man vow a vow unto the Lord, or swear an oath to bind his soul with a bond, he shall not break his word, he shall do according to all that proceeds out of his mouth." Why are people asked to take oaths before they take important public offices? Why are we asked to swear to tell the truth in court with a "so help me God" attached to it? Evidently, we as a culture know that something binding happens when we take an oath or a vow and that it is very bad karma to break such a commitment. Why? What is the unspoken truth behind that generally accepted point of view in our society? We know that the soul is bound with a bond, as it says in the book of Numbers. That means that the soul itself will now hold us accountable and responsible for fulfilling that oath or vow, with the power of the Self behind it. By making such a solemn declaration, we actually create that form, and we power it up with the force of our eternal souls and the God-Self. That form then becomes a source of strength and power that will help us fulfill the promise we made.

When you make a prayer, you create a form in the mind of God, and that form will be filled. When we make a vow, we also create a form – but it is up to us to fill it. Prayer becomes a very active force that can help us to reach up to higher levels of functioning and stay true to them, even in difficult times. We see this most obviously in marriage. The strength of the marriage vow itself has kept many a person from breaking it. Without the vow it would be much easier for people to be unfaithful and to leave marriages. Obviously, not everyone seems to find such strength in their vows or honors them so. What they fail to realize is that unless they were guided by God to break a vow, they weaken the strength of their word immensely when they do so. There will be karma to pay for that.

How do you apply all this in your life, other than when a vow or an oath is involved? Here is a truth that can change your life, once you really understand and apply it: You can impact your future immensely if you learn to create what you want consciously in your mind and heart and then bind yourself to it. Let's use a simple example: Say you want to become a doctor. You want it in your mind and you desire it with your heart. You envision how being a doctor would look and feel and why you want it. I suggest that you then ask for divine guidance to find out if being a doctor is within God's will for you. If you get an affirmative answer, you can place your word upon it. The more powerfully you learn to place your word on a decision you make, the more that commitment will become a help and strength to get you to your goal. You could stand in the presence of God and state in all conscious clarity that, barring the guidance about this pursuit changing, you place your word on it that you will not cease to pursue this goal until it is accomplished. Then you set about making all the elements involved come about.

When you approach a task (even a very large one like becoming a doctor) with such a clear commitment, and you put your word on the line for it, you will begin to bring a power into your life and into your endeavors that you would not have previously known. You can use this tool to bring into your life anything you want. You may be wondering what that would look like when applied to the spiritual things you want. You may ask yourself, "Haven't we been told that we are not to strive to have spiritual gifts – that we are to wait patiently for what God gives us in God's own time?" So I will attempt to clarify this issue for you. When is it a good practice to set spiritual goals and strive to attain them, and when is it right to simply stand and wait?

There are certain spiritual goals you really do need to strive for and make happen. I will give you some steps to help you: 1) You need to actively seek to develop a relationship with Jesus, Mary and God. 2) You need to decide that it is the most important thing in your life and arrange your life and time accordingly. 3) You will need to do everything in your power to grow your end of that relationship through learning to meditate and pray, applying those practices every day. 4) You need to listen to the advice your priests or spiritual teachers give you regarding what else you need to do to bring this about.

When you are, in fact, doing everything we teach you to do toward achieving such a relationship, the next step is to patiently wait. In this mode you go into an attitude and state of trusting God and your teachers that they will give you what you need at the right time.

What does this look like if you are hoping for and striving toward becoming a dedicated student and having a personal spiritual teacher? Your part in bringing this about looks like you attending everything offered at your spiritual center. In addition, you need to make sure your basic life issues are in order. This includes making an income that is sufficient, being emotionally balanced enough to take on some challenging spiritual training, and being open and willing to be instructed and guided, doing all the work you are given to do. Spiritual training is not to be used as an excuse to get free therapy or an opportunity to whine and moan to an audience without doing what it takes to transform. It is entirely about change and growth and learning to move beyond your own issues to be able to be of service to others. If you are too caught up in your own world to have any interest in service to others, then you need therapy, not spiritual training. If you are not willing to move beyond your anger and pain and into love and forgiveness, you also don't need in-depth spiritual training. If you are wed to being negative and critical in your thinking and to tearing others down in your heart and mind, why would it make any sense for a teacher to try to teach you the way of love? If you barely do the work that is given you to do and barely show up, then you are making your teachers drag you, and frankly, most teachers have better things to do with their time.

You also need to be working on ridding yourself of the fears you hold inside which prevent you from accepting the light. These fears could include that of masculine energy, or men, or authority figures. These are fears, which will keep you from allowing the Master Jesus to approach you and fill you with light or keep you from allowing us to work that closely with you to bring the light into you. You may also have fears of surrendering to God so completely and giving up the control you have allowed your head to keep over your life.

Once you are doing all those things faithfully, then you can practice patience and trust in God and your teachers to bring the gifts of progress and initiation to you when the time is right. Remember, that can be at quite different times for different people. I want everyone to come into the graces that Jesus and Mary have for us humans as soon as is possibly right for them. So I would never hold someone back. But some people create great obstacles and thereby take significantly more time than others to move along the path. It is wrong vis-à-vis Jesus and Mary to demand their graces. We need to be open, willing, obedient and patient, humbly seeking to draw ever closer to them, allowing them to choose what is right for us.

I had to wait almost seven years after my mystical baptism to come into illumination, and twelve years after becoming a deacon to be ordained a priest. I am not saying that any of you necessarily need to wait that long for your next steps, but rather sometimes that is what God has in store for some of us. I learned a lot while waiting for what I wanted most to come about. So will you whenever you are patiently waiting for God to give you the next step. But remember, that is not a passive state of waiting, but rather a very active time of inner and outer work. Some of the most important lessons I learned were ones that directly prepared me to run a spiritual order. So this time of waiting was very active in a way I could not have understood at the time. Now, years later, I am so grateful for God's wisdom in teaching me during those years what I now can put to such good use.

What if you feel a calling to be a minister or a priest? How can you help bring that about? You will need to know which order or denomination you would want to serve with. You will need to find the teachers and school that will teach you. Above all, you will want to get as clear as you possibly can that this is God's will for you. If it is your will without it being God's will, it could have disastrous consequences for you and for others. Once you feel sure you want to move in that direction and you know through which congregation you want to be trained and ordained, you will need to very actively remove everything from your life, heart, and mind that would come between you and the ministry. Through the cleaning out of those things that are not useful to your growth and service to God, you will create a void. Then you will be able to fill that void with an ever-increasing amount of light and with the presence and connectedness to God that you will need to function as God's emissary. When you do, you will be able to take on that authority and that love.

You will have plenty of inner and outer work to do, as you wait patiently for God to determine the right time to empower you through ordination. This time to stand and wait comes when you have done all that is in your power toward what you are striving for and it is now up to God to determine when you should be brought into that next step. This stage of the process develops important spiritual muscles in us. We can practice the virtues of humility, trusting in God and our teachers, being in the present, and relaxing. These skills are at least as important as the skills we use when we are in active mode.

What if your experience is more the reverse, where you feel surprised and perhaps not ready when the invitation into the ministry comes to you sooner than you had expected? Once again, it will be a matter of you setting about doing all the work you need to do to be prepared for that calling. In this case, the trusting aspect will come not in waiting but in knowing that God knows when things are right for you, even if they are faster than what you thought you were ready for. Can you trust God and your teachers enough to let God's will come through at whatever speed God chooses to deliver it? If your answer is yes and you are actively willing to do the work needed to transform yourself and your habitual ways of acting, thinking, and feeling, then you will be well on the way to becoming useful in the great plan God has for this planet. Then Jesus and Mary can look at you with joy, knowing that they have another worker to use in the harvest of bringing souls to the life, the light, and the love of God.

I am exhorting you to take charge of your life. Decide what you want to bring into your life, and set about making that happen. Remember, it will take cleaning out all your old patterns and ways of doing things that are no longer useful. It will take establishing new ones that are in accord with God, Jesus, and Mary. And it will take using your ability to establish ties that bind you to those new commitments and making them firm so they can be the support structure that helps you to arrive at your goals. Philippians 2: 5 states, "Let this mind be in you that was also in Christ Jesus, who, being in the form of God, thought it not robbery to be equal to God."

Let us not consider it robbery to strive to be completely whole and full of the power that God has given us to bind and loosen from us all those things that are right to be bound and loosened. Let us not consider it blasphemy to strive to do exactly as Jesus taught, to be that committed and that empowered to change the world in and around us. May God bless you in your work to come into such a state of wholeness and in your developing commitment that helps bring such wholeness to others.

CHAPTER NINE

In God We Live and Move and Have Our Being

Thou must be emptied of that wherewith thou art full,
that thou mayest be filled with that whereof thou art empty.

~ Saint Augustine

In preceding sections of this book, I have given the spiritual anatomy of the God-Self residing in the soul, which is in the vicinity of the solar plexus. You may know various teachings about the God-Self from other teachers and from reading spiritual books. But what do you actually know from your experience? What does it mean to have God living within you? How does this affect your life, and what is God doing in there, anyhow?

When we try to think about God within us, we have great difficulty because we are using a very limited tool to try to understand a very vast reality. It is as if we were using a small toy telescope to comprehend the vastness of the universe. We could only see the planets somewhat magnified. We could not even see our own Milky Way galaxy very well. With that small tool, we could only get a bit of an idea that there must be much more out there. It is just like that when we try to think about the God within us. It is actually fine that we cannot comprehend it any more than that. We can think and understand enough information to know where to look and focus our attention on coming into a real experience of the Self. It is actually not our thinking minds that draw us toward the Self. It is the desire in our hearts that comes from the soul. That desire is what tells us that there is a union that is possible between us and God within and that this union will be greater than anything that has ever been known to us. Our soul creates the longing, the draw, and the pull to find that state of union, no matter what it takes to get there. Our mind contributes by learning to concentrate, focus, and give up its demand to control our lives.

Now imagine being that God-Self inside of you. Imagine that you are a being and that you live in the center of a physical body. Imagine that you are only a soul and a Self and that you wear a physical body like an outer garment. Between you and that outer garment is the spiritual body that connects you with the body. So there you are, soul and Self, as you have always been for thousands of years. You took on this particular physical body a number of years ago. You had it built to suit your needs for this incarnation. With the help of spiritual guides, you decided before incarnating whether you needed to be male or female, tall or short, which race, which features and all the other details of your physical form. You decided what family you needed, what astrological influences you should come under, and when you should come into that body.

You also decided what you wanted to achieve in this life. It was with this in mind that you chose all the other details of your incarnation. You and your spiritual guides agreed on the areas you needed to develop and what kind of circumstances would optimize your chances of doing so. And because you are reading this book, I know you may also have asked that you find an inner mystical school and that you would be given the chance to train and to serve humanity through such a school. You may have indicated that you very much wanted to find teachers that could bring you into the light and into the presence of God. It was your soul's deep desire, and God answers all our prayers. So the fact that you are reading this book may well have a much longer history than you imagined. You may also have decided in a previous lifetime that you wanted to commit for the rest of all your lives on earth to be of service to God and humankind. In such a case, you have eternal vows on your soul and the means to fulfill those vows was built into the plans for your incarnation.

So imagine that after all that careful planning, you incarnate into the body you had built and into the family and circumstances you chose. Initially, you are there in a body that can't do anything for itself except eat, make some sounds, squirm and eliminate waste. You look out through the eyes that are just learning to focus and you listen with ears that are just beginning to know how to discern differences in sounds and direction. You know you are completely dependent on your caregivers to keep you alive. There you are, a full-blown soul and God-Self, in the little body of a baby. Then you begin the journey through the first seven years of getting the body to do everything you need it to do. If all is going reasonably well in your life, you spend the second seven years getting the conscious mind to be able to reason, focus and concentrate. And if after you have been in this body for about fourteen years and your family and environment has allowed you to develop fairly normally, you begin working on your emotional development.

If all is more or less on schedule, by the time this body you wear is approximately 21 years old, your outer being will begin to look for a relationship with God; that is what ages 21 to 28 are really for. However, most people encounter some problems along the way and may find they need extra years to develop the physical, reasoning and emotional areas of their

beings. When that is the case, those are the topics that domi-
nate the years to come. If, however, those needs of the body,
emotions and mind are at least somewhat adequately met, you
– that is your soul and Self – will be able to get through to your
outer being, reminding it that there is more to accomplish in
this body than just the satisfaction of those needs. You will
begin, from the inside out, to put pressure on your thinking
and feeling. You will work valiantly at getting through to your
outer parts. You will try to get the attention of your body, mind
and heart to remind them of the greater plan for your life.

What you, the soul-Self, often finds is that these aspects of your
outer functioning, with so many years to develop, have now
taken on a life of their own. The thinking and feeling functions
have forgotten that they were just tools for you to use and express through, and they have instead declared that they are
you. They now run around the world impersonating you and
actually forgetting you exist. They seek to meet their needs in
the outer world and cut off all contact from you. Here the great
tragedy happens: You now believe your soul to be a question-
ably existent part of your outer being, rather than who you really are. And it is no longer heard or sought out. You may have
speculated about it but declared it to be unknowable. You may
have spoken of it but not allowed it to speak. And you have
come to believe that the pure God that you, the soul, hold at
your core, is outside somewhere, if you believe it to exist at all.

How did this happen? This outer part of you, which was allowed to develop and to be a means through which you, the
soul, could interact with the world, has taken over. Those
parts, which were meant to be developed so that they could
turn inward and join with you, the soul-Self, have declared
they do not know you. Those parts, which were to join with
you, the inner being, in an ecstatic embrace have joined with
the outer world instead. You, the eternal, beautiful soul-Self,
are unseen, unloved and abandoned. You who has the whole

love of God to offer to your outer being, who wants to give to it all knowledge, all wisdom, all ecstasy and bliss, is ignored and passed over for difficult and, at best, only partially satisfying love relationships with people outside of yourself. Everything you, as soul, have to give and share is seen as worthless compared to the outer possibilities of the world. So you remain alone, not being acknowledged, with no one to give your love to and no one to share the blessings of heaven with.

In the meantime, the outer parts of you, your thinking and emotions, are looking everywhere for love and satisfaction of all their desires. They go through heartbreak after heartbreak and false hope after false hope trying to find the one great love that will make everything in life okay. They try to fill their hunger with material objects and with success and achievement. They go to everything and everywhere looking for love, meaning, satisfaction and peace. They look everywhere except turning inward to you, the soul-Self. They get depressed and discouraged, while there you are, the inner being, the one who could give them everything, is ignored, abandoned, unseen, and unacknowledged. Your life in this incarnation then comes to an end, the soul and Self leave the body to its destiny to return to the elements of earth, and they look back on this life and see they missed the boat. This is the tragedy of the vast majority of human beings' existence on Earth.

I am now going to ask you to switch to a completely different perspective. Imagine now how God, creator of heaven and earth, decided to create humans. As God's consciousness and mind fill our entire solar system, everything in this solar system is within God. God then experiences us within God's own being as a part of God's self. So within God's own being, God created individual human beings to whom God gave the right to choose what they want to do with their lives. God conceived each soul in love and in beauty and then gave each one its freedom to decide when each one wanted to come back into a state of love and union with God. God created each soul for the purpose of having them find their way back to God, knowing that many of them would choose to stay away for some time. This brought sorrow to God because God knew that they would be sad and lost being away from God's love and guidance. But God also knew that love that is not voluntary is not worth much. God wanted us to come back into a loving and knowing relationship with God when we felt ready. And God is willing to wait for thousands of years, if that is how long we choose to spend away from our source of peace and love.

You were created as a soul within God's own being, and from that time forward you have continued to live inside of God. Are you actually aware of that? All around you is God. You move inside of God, you breathe in God, you walk on God. You also think into God's mind, which is why your thoughts create. Your emotions move out into the substance of God's being. You have never been out of that embrace and total care of God for one moment of your existence. And when you die, you will leave your body and continue existing within that being that is God. This is not my personal philosophy; it is straight from the New Testament. The Apostle Paul wrote, "God in whom we live and move and have our beings." How much clearer could Paul have put it? It was written in other places that God is closer than your hands and your feet, closer than your breath.

So what happened? How did we then come to feel like God is nowhere, or at least far away? God gave us the ability to think with our conscious minds whatever we wanted. Back in the Garden of Eden, Eve and Adam walked in the presence of God. They lived fully in God, represented by God's garden, which gave them everything they needed. They were at peace with themselves and each other and spoke openly with God all the time. They were naked, meaning they had no defenses or shame or barriers between them and God, and it never even occurred to them to cover themselves and hide from God.

Eve can be seen as representing the soul and Adam as representing consciousness, the consciousness that was given to each soul. It is the inner original consciousness that connects to the mind of God and is fully aware.

Your original state when God made you was just like Eve's, your soul was alive and fully manifesting in the world free to be itself and express without fear or shame. Its primary desire was for God, and it was united with your consciousness, represented by Adam, in a pure and harmonious union. You knew that you lived within God's own being and that you were completely taken care of. You knew that whenever you reached out for something it would be there. You knew the presence of God and found your joy in communicating with it, "walking in the garden with God." Your consciousness brought your attention to things that needed to be focused on and brought them to you, the soul, to take in and bring into the presence of God. Then God, soul and consciousness all walked together, and God brought ever deeper wisdom and depth to your being.

Muslims have the same word for a person's lower nature and for Satan. Satan, or if you prefer, your lower nature, brought up the temptation in you that changed everything. You may say, "Where did the lower nature come from?" You were made with the freedom to do anything. So one cannot call it freedom if one could not also choose to do things of a lower nature. So at some point, each of us was presented with the thought, "Wouldn't you like to be like God, as great, as powerful, as beautiful as God?" Now, if you contemplate that question, you will see that in order to compete with God in such a way you would have to first be separate from God. You cannot be in the awareness of being in God and God being in you and simultaneously be competing with God. So first the temptation to compete with God is presented to your desire nature (Eve), the lower feminine part of you. The desire nature can be pure and want just God or it can drop low and want to be God, outside of God, better than God.

Once the desire has dropped to that level, it approaches consciousness. Consciousness, represented by Adam, was vast and clear and completely operating within God's consciousness. The temptation the lower desire nature presented to your consciousness was that you could have a mind of your own and then be smarter than God, making all your decisions yourself. You could then become the king of your own universe. Being prideful came up for both Eve and Adam as each, desire and consciousness, contemplated having their own world in which they ruled together. Genesis tells us that Eve took a bite of the apple and gave it to Adam. It goes on to say that soon thereafter God came strolling along as God always did. When Adam and Eve heard God coming, they were afraid, because they were naked. And they took fig leaves and covered their nakedness before God.

Why were they now afraid? Why were they now ashamed of their nakedness? They were ashamed because they were now using their separate faculties of conscious mind thinking and their emotions. They had successfully made the split from the soul and the greater consciousness, which had been always in the presence of God. Now the presence was separate and scary. They became afraid of God for the first time. And in that fear they then experienced God as judging and condemning, and they experienced God as casting them out of God's presence, the Garden of Eden. In the separate experience they now entered into, Adam had to work in sweat and dirt just to make ends meet. Eve had to give birth in pain. They experienced intercourse as animals did, a need to propagate and satisfy the body's needs. Before that they had come together in a union of soul and consciousness in ecstatic oneness with God. But they wanted to be separate and to control their own world.

This is how your thinking and emotions separated off from the soul and consciousness within you and began to do their own thing. You have now for eons believed that you are, in fact, those two things: Your thoughts and your emotions. In each lifetime, each of us has had to do at least a miniature version of Adam and Eve's journey again. We go from infancy, a time in which we are completely open to God to when we begin to think around age seven and then begin to develop our emotions around age 14. As teenagers, we separate off and demand independence. After we turn 21, we begin to look once again for the union we feel we once knew within our own beings, the union we once knew with God. If all goes well, by the time we are 28, we will firmly have our feet back on the path to that union.

Do you now see why we tell you that God doesn't go away from us, only we go away from God? Once we separate ourselves in our thinking and emotions from God, then we experience God as the one who is making us have so much pain. We believe God is punishing us, and we keep moving farther away. And yet, in truth, we are still within the being of God. God is still all around us. We are still in the Garden of Eden because all our needs are still being met by God, once we recognize God as the source of all. We can still be walking with God and have no shame of our nakedness and no fear of the presence. All of these things are still there when we sink deep inside ourselves and are on the level of our soul and our greater consciousness.

Imagine once again what all this feels like from God's perspective. Here we are, God's creatures, alive within God's mind, heart and consciousness, part of God's body, and yet we disconnect so much with that reality that each of us acts like we are our own separate universe. So we fight and compete with each other and with God. We don't go to God for help. We look for all our satisfaction from other sources. And we even proclaim God does not exist or is mean and stupid. God allows all this to transpire within God's own being because of God's infinite love for us. God allows us all the time we need or want to decide to return to the Garden of Eden.

Why was Jesus called the second Adam and Mary the second Eve? Because Jesus and Mary broke the patterns that Adam and Eve established. Mary chose to have her desire and soul focused entirely on God and on her love for God. Just think of her canticle, "My soul doth magnify the Lord." She never separated, never moved out of oneness with God and into wanting her own thing. Jesus kept his consciousness right there with God. When the devil tempted him in the desert to have his own earthly kingdom, to use his powers for himself and to be adored as a separate person from God, he refused. You have within you the same choices. You have that soul and desire nature that can want only God or can want to boost your pride and yourself as a separate creature. You also have in you that consciousness that can stay united with the mind and heart of God and let God flow through you. You can live "Thy will be done" or you can do your own separate thing.

Do you now understand a bit more that you truly are in God and God in you? Can you now open yourself just a little to enter into that reality and begin to live and move in it? Are you willing to open to God's love and return to a state of union with God, or do you still have to have it your way? Do you trust God enough to take your foot off the brakes that control your rate of growth and development and just let God move you as God sees fit? When will you be ready to let God call you back to God's self to be in oneness with God's will for you?

If you want to adopt this understanding, you will need to work on it daily. You will need to constantly correct yourself when you find yourself acting and thinking as if you were separate from God. You will need to constantly tune back into the truth that you are in God, God is in you, and God is all you need. This is cosmic consciousness, Christ consciousness, Buddha consciousness, or whatever else you would like to call it. It is oneness with God. And it is entirely up to you whether you enter it or not. For God already has you in God's being and consciousness. The question is only when will you join God there. May God within you and God all around you bless your journey home to God.

Mystical Roses of Peace

CHAPTER TEN

Mother Mary: A Powerful and Loving Reality for Today's Spiritual Seeker

For she is a reflection of eternal light, a spotless mirror
of the working of God, and an image of [the Lord's] goodness.
Although she is but one, she can do all things,
and while remaining in herself, she renews all things;
in every generation she passes into holy souls
and makes them friends of God, and prophets;
for God loves nothing so much
as the person who lives with Sophia/Wisdom.

~ Wisdom of Solomon 7:26-28

I welcome you warmly into this contemplation of Mother Mary, whether you are a person who already relates to and loves her or whether you are newly beginning to learn about her. My prayer is that you will have a deeper and fuller connection with her by the end of this chapter.

Mother Mary is not only a historical figure, not only an archetype of the Divine Feminine, and not only the one who immaculately conceived, gave birth to, and was the teacher of the greatest being the earth has ever seen. Though she is all of these, in addition, Mother Mary is also a living reality with whom anyone who so wishes can connect. I will begin by introducing Mother Mary to you as I have come to know her. If you care enough to put in the effort and love, you can develop a deep, rewarding and transforming relationship with her. Although I will speak a little about Mary as a historical figure and as the mother of Jesus, my focus will address who she can become in your life, if you want her to hold such a role for you. As such, the heart of this chapter will be devoted to the living reality aspect of Mother Mary.

Let's begin with some background on Mother Mary. The New Testament has very little information about her. Fortunately, several visionaries have been shown many details about Mary's life, so we are not left bereft of information about her birth and her life. The best sources are Maria Valtorta's five volumes called *The Poem of the Man-God* and Anne Catherine Emmerich's *The Life of the Blessed Virgin*. Both authors were devout Catholic nuns who were given ongoing, in-depth visions of the lives of Jesus and Mary. They offer inspired and uplifting readings, which I highly recommend. From these writings we learn that Mother Mary's parents were deeply devoted to God and were already advanced in age when they became her parents. They longed for a child and finally were granted the answer to that prayer. Mary was conceived immaculately, meaning her parents did not conceive her through intercourse but rather through the infusion of the Holy Spirit into her mother, Anna. Anna and her husband, Joachim, agreed to give back to God this daughter, whom they had longed and hoped for and finally received. When Mary was three years old, her parents brought her to the temple and to be raised as a temple virgin in service to God. From a very young age Mary expressed her desire to grow up in the temple. In the follow-

---

[1] Maria Valtorta. *The Poem of the Man-God* (Isola del Liri: Centro Editoriale Valtortiano srl, 2003). Text references are to author, volume and page number.

ing quote from Valtorta's *The Poem of the Man-God*[1] , you get a sense of her as a three-year-old child in this conversation with her mother:

> "I want to always be like this flower and like the wise king I want to sing throughout My life canticles and prayers before the Tabernacle," says Mary.
>
> "How do You know these holy things? Who told You? Your father?"
>
> "No. I don't know who it is. I think I have always known them. Perhaps there is one who tells Me and I do not see him. Perhaps one of the angels that God sends to speak to good people. Mummy, will you tell me another story?"
>
> "Oh, my dear, which story do You wish to know?"
>
> Mary is thinking, deeply absorbed in Her thoughts. Her expression should be immortalized in a portrait. The shadows of Her thoughts are reflected on Her childish face. There are smiles and sighs, sunshine and clouds, thinking of the history of Israel. Then She makes up Her mind: "Once again the story of Gabriel and Daniel, where Christ is promised."
>
> And She listens, with Her eyes closed, repeating in a low voice the words Her mother says, as if to remember them better. When Anne comes to the end Mary asks: "How long will it be before we have the Immanuel?"
>
> "About thirty years, my darling."
>
> "Such a long time! And I shall be in the Temple ... Tell Me, if I should pray very hard, so hard, day and

night, night and day, and I wanted to belong only to God, for all my life, for this purpose, would the Eternal Father grant Me the grace of sending the Messiah to His people sooner?"

"I do not know, my dear. The Prophet states: "Seventy weeks." I do not think a prophecy can be wrong. But the Lord is so good" she hastens to add, seeing tears appear on the fair eyelashes of her child, "the Lord is so good that I believe that if You do pray very hard, so hard, He will hear Your prayers."

A smile appears once again on Her little face, which She has lifted up to Her mother and the rays of the sun, filtering through the vine branches cause Her tears to shine like dew-drops on very thin stems of alpine moss.

"Then I will pray and I shall be a virgin for this."

"But do you know what that means?"

"It means that one does not know human love, but only the love of God. It means that one has no other thought but for the Lord. It means to remain children of the flesh and angels in the heart. It means that one has eyes but to look to God, and ears to listen to Him, and a mouth to praise Him, hands to offer oneself as a victim, feet to follow Him fast, and a heart and life to be given to Him."

"May God bless you! But then you will never have children, and yet You love babies and little lambs and doves so much ... Do You know that? A baby is for his mother like a little white and curly lamb, he is like a dove with silk feathers and coral mouth to be loved and kissed and heard say: 'Mummy!'"

"It does not matter. I shall belong to God. I shall pray in the Temple. And perhaps one day I will see the Immanuel. The Virgin who is to be His Mother must already be born, as the great Prophet says, and She is in the Temple ... I will be Her companion ... and maidservant. Oh! Yes. If I could only meet Her, by God's light, I would like to serve Her, the Blessed One. And later, She would bring Me Her Son, She would take Me to Her Son, and I would serve Him too ... Just think, mummy! ... To serve the Messiah!" Mary is overcome by this thought that exalts Her and makes Her totally humble at the same time. With Her hands crossed over Her breast and Her little head slightly bent forward and flushed with emotion, She is like an infantile reproduction of the Annunciation that I saw. She resumes: "But will the King of Israel, the Lord's Anointed, allow Me to serve Him?"

"Have no doubt about that. Does King Solomon not say: 'There are sixty queens and eighty concubines and countless maidens?' You can see that in the King's palace there will be countless maidens serving the Lord."

"Oh! You can see then that I must be a virgin? I must. If He wants a virgin as His Mother, it means He loves virginity above all things. I want Him to love Me, His maiden, because of the virginity, which will make me somewhat like His beloved Mother. This is what I want..." (Valtorta, 1, 38-40)

Shortly after, Joachim, Mary's father comes in and she makes the following request:

"Oh, Daddy, when are you taking Me to the Temple?"

"Soon, my dear. But are you not sorry to leave

Your father?"

"Yes, very much! But you will come ...in any case, if it did not hurt, what sacrifice would it be?"

"And will you always remember us?"

"I always will. After the prayer for the Immanuel, I will pray for you. That God may give you joy and a long life ... until the day He becomes the Savior. Then I will ask Him to take you to the celestial Jerusalem."

The vision ends with Mary clasped tightly in Her father's arms. (Valtorta, 1, 40-41)

From this reading, have you gotten a sense of the beauty of this soul named Mary? Even the little child Mary has so much to teach us that she could provide us with a lifetime of devotional focus and example. At age three, Mary dedicated herself to the highest service to God that she could imagine, which was to ask God to speed up the time of the coming of the Christ through her unceasing prayers. She knew that the incarnation of Christ would be the turning point for all humankind. She gave over all wants for her own life to help bring about this gift for others. She set about being perfectly pure in her every thought, emotion, action and word. By giving herself so completely to this cause, she hoped to bring about enough grace to speed up the coming of the healing power of the Christ for all people. By giving up her parents, that which a 3-year-old loves the most and is the most afraid to lose, she sacrificed everything she had for her love for other people.

The following is Mary as a 14-year-old girl in the temple:

While Mary is getting up after Her prayer, with ecstatic brightness still on Her face, old Anna of Phanuel enters the room. She stands still, amazed or at least wondering at Mary's attitude and appearance.

Then she calls Her: "Mary!" and the girl turns round with a smile, a different one but still so beautiful and says: "Peace to you, Anna."

"Were You praying? Are Your prayers never enough for You?"

"My prayers would be enough. But I speak to God. Anna, you cannot imagine how close I feel to Him. More than close, within My heart. May God forgive my pride. But I don't feel lonely. See? Over there, in that House of gold and snow, behind the Curtain, there is the Holy of Holies. Nobody is ever allowed to look at the Propitiatory, on which the glory of the Lord rests, except the High Priest. But my worshipping soul does not need to look at the embroidered Curtain, which quivers at the songs of the virgins and Levites and is scented with precious incense, as if I wanted to pierce its fabric and see the Testimony shine through it. I do look at it! Do not think that I do not look at it with worshipping eyes like every son of Israel. Do not think that pride blinds Me making Me think what I will now tell you. I look at it and there is no more humble servant among the people of God that looks more humbly at the House of the Lord than I do, because I am convinced that I am the least of all. But what do I see? A veil. What do you think is behind the Veil? A Tabernacle. What is in it? I listen to My heart, I see God shining in His loving glory and He says to Me: "I love You" and I reply to Him: "I love You" and I die and I am recreated at each beat of My heart in this reciprocal kiss...I am amongst you, My dear teachers and companions. But a circle of fire isolates Me from you. Within the circle, God and Myself. And I see you through the Fire of God and so I love you ... but I cannot love you according to the flesh, neither shall I ever be able to love anyone according to the flesh. I can only love Him Who loves Me, according to the spirit. This is My destiny. The secular Law of Israel wants every girl to be a wife, and every wife a mother. But, while obeying the Law, I must obey the Voice that whispers to Me: "I want You;" I am a virgin and a virgin I shall remain. How shall I succeed? This sweet invisible Presence that is with Me will help Me, because it is Its desire. I am not afraid. I have no longer father and mother ... and only God knows how My love for whatever human being belonged to Me was burnt in that pain. Now I have but God. I therefore obey Him unquestioningly ... I would have done so also regardless of My father and mother, because I have been taught by the Voice that whoever wishes to follow It, must go beyond father and mother. Parents are loving patrols watching the hearts of their children, whom they wish to lead to happiness according to their plans ... and they are not aware of other plans leading to infinite happiness ... I would have left them my dresses and mantles to follow the Voice that says to me: "Come, My beloved Spouse". I would have left them everything, and the pearls of My tears, for I would have cried for having to disobey them, and the instincts of My blood, because I would have defied even death to follow the Voice calling Me, would have told them that there is something greater and sweeter than the love of a father and mother and that is the Voice of God. But now, by His will, I am free of all filial love ... I am My own guide on earth, or rather God guides His poor servant giving Her His commands and I fulfill them because it is a joy to me to obey." (Valtorta, 1, 52-53)

Can you imagine having the kind of relationship with God that the young Mary describes here? God is her beloved, her one and only love, with whom she spends time, and whose love woos her and fills her and gives her superhuman joy. She is so thoroughly wed to God that she feels it would be impossible to ever give herself into a human relationship. Do you now see why God chose her to be God's bride, the one into whom God would infuse God's self to bring about the conception of God's son? Her heart belonged entirely to God, and her only desire was to help her suffering fellow humans by praying that the Messiah come sooner to alleviate their pain. She had no thought for herself. All her love was for God and humankind. She was entirely selfless, and as a result, entirely available to God to bring God's grace to earth.

The next vision from Valtorta is as follows:

> What I see: Mary, a very young girl: She looks fifteen years old, at most. She is in a small rectangular room: a room most suitable for a girl. Along one of the longer walls, there is a bed: a low bed, without bedstead, covered with thick mats or carpets ... Beside the bookcase, towards the door, which opens onto the kitchen garden and which is now covered by a curtain gently moved by a light breeze, there is the Virgin sitting on a low stool. She is spinning some linen which is white as snow and as soft as silk. Her little hands, just a little darker than linen, are whirling the spindle very quickly. Her beautiful young face is slightly bent forward and She is smiling gently as if She were caressing or following some sweet thought.
>
> There is a great silence in the little house and in the kitchen garden. There is a great peace both on Mary's face and in the surrounding place. There is peace and order. Everything is neat and tidy and the room, though very modest looking, has something austere and regal about it because of its cleanliness and the care with which everything is laid ... Mary be-

gins to sing in a low voice ... The song changes into a prayer: "Most High God, do not delay any longer in sending Your Servant to bring peace to the world. Grant us the favorable time and the pure and prolific virgin for the coming of Your Christ. Father, Holy Father, grant Me, Your servant to offer My life for this purpose. Grant Me to die after seeing Your Light and Your Justice on earth and after knowing that our Redemption has been accomplished. Oh Holy Father, send the Promise of the Prophets to the earth. Send the Redeemer to Your maidservant, so that in the hour of My death, Your abode may be opened to Me. Come, come, Oh Spirit of the Lord. Come to the faithful who are expecting You. Come, Prince of Peace!" Mary remains absorbed thus.

The curtain moves fast, as if someone behind it ventilated it or shook it to draw it. And a pearl of white light mixed with pure silver makes the slightly yellow walls clearer and makes the colors of the cloths brighter and Mary's raised face more spiritual. And in such light, while the curtain is still drawn on the mystery to be accomplished, the Archangel prostrates himself: the curtain no longer moves ...

The Angel must necessarily take a human appearance. But it is a transhumanised appearance. Of what flesh is this beautiful and gleaming figure made? With what substance did God form it to make it perceptible to the senses of the Virgin? Only God can possess such substances and use them so perfectly. It is a face, a body, eyes, a mouth, hair and hands like ours. But they are not our dull matter. It is a light that has taken color of flesh, of eyes, hair, lips, and light that moves and smiles, looks and speaks.

"Hail, Mary, full of Grace, Hail!" The voice is a

sweet arpeggio as of pearls thrown on a precious metal plate.

Mary is startled and lowers Her head. And She is even more startled when She sees the shining creature kneeling about a meter from Her and looking at Her with infinite veneration, his hands crossed over his chest.

Mary jumps to Her feet and She squeezes against the wall. She turns pale and red alternately. Her face shows surprise and fear. She subconsciously presses Her hands against Her breast hiding them under Her long sleeves. She stoops, endeavoring to conceal Her body as much as possible. An attitude of gentle modesty.

"No. Do not fear. The Lord is with you! You are blessed amongst all women!"

But Mary continues to be afraid. Where has that extraordinary being come from? Is he a messenger of God or of the Deceiver?

"Do not fear, Mary!" repeats the Archangel. "I am Gabriel, the Angel of God. My Lord has sent me to You. Do not be afraid, because You have found grace in the eyes of God. And You will conceive and bear a Son and You will call Him 'Jesus': He will be great and will be called Son of the Most High (and such He will really be). And the Lord God will give Him the throne of His Ancestor David and He will rule over the House of Jacob forever and His reign will have no end. Understand, Oh Holy Virgin loved by God, Daughter blessed by God, called to be the Mother of His Son, what Son you will generate!"

"How can this come about, since I do not know

man? Perhaps the Lord God will no longer accept the offer of His maidservant and does not want Me a Virgin for His love?"

"Not by deed of man You will be a mother, Mary. You are the eternal Virgin, the Holy Virgin of God. The Holy Spirit will come upon You and the power of the Most High will cover You with its shadow. So the child born of You will be called Holy and the Son of God ... Nothing is impossible to the Lord, Mary, full of Grace. What shall I tell my Lord? Let no thought whatsoever disturb You. He will protect Your interests if You trust in Him. The world, Heaven, and the Eternal Father are awaiting Your word!"

Mary crosses Her hands over Her breast and bowing down deeply, She says: "I am the handmaid of the Lord. Let what you have said be done to Me.'"

The Angel shines out of joy. He kneels in adoration because he certainly sees the Spirit of God descend upon the Virgin bent down in assent, and he disappears without moving the curtain, but leaves it well drawn over the holy Mystery. (Valtorta, 1, 79-82)

All of Mary's preparation to serve God was found holy in God's sight and was fulfilled when the Angel Gabriel came to her. She gave us the eternal words: "Behold the handmaiden of God. Let it be done unto Me according to Your word." Take a moment and try to imagine what state you would need to be in to speak those words and mean them with your entire self. You could only do that if you had absolute and complete trust in God and a total dedication to doing only what God wants, no matter what the cost to you and your ideas and plans. It is a phrase I recommend that you meditate on and ask for help to grow into such a state of grace.

The next episode is when Mary and Joseph are in the stable the night of Jesus' birth:

"Are You not sleeping, Mary?" asks Joseph.

He asks Her three times until She turns around and replies: "I am praying."

"Is there anything You need?"

"No, Joseph."

"Try and sleep a little. At least try and rest."

"I will try. But I do not get tired praying."

"God be with You, Mary."

"And with you, Joseph.'"

Mary resumes Her position. Joseph, to avoid falling asleep, goes on his knees near the fire and prays. He prays with his hands pressed against his face. He removes them now and again to feed the fire and then he resumes his ardent prayer. Apart from the noise of the crackling sticks and the noise made now and again by the donkey stamping its hooves on the ground, no other sound is heard.

A thin ray of moonlight creeps in through a crack in the vault and it seems a blade of unearthly silver looking for Mary. It stretches in length as the moon climbs higher in the sky and at last reaches her. It is now on Her head, where it forms a halo of pure light.

Mary lifts Her head, as if She had a celestial call, and She gets up and goes on Her knees again. Oh! How beautiful it is here now! She raises Her head, and

Her face shines in the white moonlight and becomes transfigured by a supernatural smile. What does She see? What does She hear? What does She feel? She is the only one who can tell what She saw, heard and felt in the refulgent hour of Her Maternity. I can only see that the light around Her is increasing more and more. It seems to come down from Heaven, to arise from the poor things around Her, above all it seems to originate from Herself.

Her deep blue dress now seems pale blue, and Her hands and face are becoming clear blue as if they were placed under the glare of a huge, pale sapphire. This hue is spreading more and more on the things around Her, it covers them, purifies them and brightens everything ... The light is given off more and more intensely from Mary's body, it absorbs the moonlight. She seems to be drawing to Herself all the light that can descend from Heaven. She is now the Depository of the Light. She is to give this Light to the world. And this blissful, uncontainable, immeasurable, eternal, divine Light which is about to be given, is heralded by dawn, a morning star, a chorus of atoms of Light that increase continuously like a tide, and rise more and more like incense, and descend like a large stream and stretch out like veils ...

The vault, full of crevices, of cobwebs, of protruding rubble balanced by a miracle of physics, the dark, smoky repellant vault, now seems the ceiling of a royal hall. Each boulder is a block of silver, each crack an opal flash, each cobweb a most precious canopy interwoven with silver and diamonds ... And the light increases more and more. It is now unbearable to the eye. And the Virgin disappears in so much light, as if She had been absorbed by an incandescent curtain ... and the Mother emerges.

Yes, when the light becomes endurable once again to my eyes, I see Mary with the newborn Son in Her arms. A little Baby, rosy and plump, bustling with His hands as big as rose buds and kicking with His tiny feet that could be contained in the hollow of the heart of a rose; and is crying with a thin trembling voice, just like a newborn lamb, opening His pretty little mouth ... And He moves His little head that is so blond that it seems without any hair, a round head that His Mummy holds in the hollow of Her hand, while She looks at Her Baby and adores Him weeping and smiling at the same time, and She bends down to kiss Him not on His innocent head, but on the center of His chest, where underneath there is His little heart beating for us ... where one day there will be the Wound. And His Mother is doctoring that wound in advance, with Her immaculate kiss.

[Joseph rouses and he and Mary] meet at the foot of the straw bed and they look at each other, weeping blissfully. "Come, let us offer Jesus to the Father" says Mary. And while Joseph kneels down, She stands up ... lifts up Her Creature in Her arms and says: "Here I am. On His behalf, Oh God, I speak these words to You: here I am to do Your will. And I, Mary, and My spouse, Joseph, with Him. Here are Your servants, 0 Lord. May Your will always be done by us, in every hour, in every event, for Your glory and Your love." (Valtorta, 1, 139-141)

Remember, Mother Mary was still only about sixteen years old. What can we learn from her through these stories of her preparation for the coming of God into her being and her giving birth to God? It is clearly endearing to hear of all her dedication and love, but how can you apply it?

This chapter consists primarily of stories. Why? It is because

Mother Mary works less through our intellect and more through our hearts. The easiest way to begin to know her and open to her is to hear stories about her and feel how she was when on earth. As your heart is moved through the stories, begin to open to the possibility of experiencing her presence as she is now. In many ways, she is still the same now as she was then. She is so simple in her complete love of God and humans. She is so pure in her dedication to service. And she is still as humble as always, even though she now carries titles such as Queen of Heaven and Mother of God. How can she be humble with such titles? It is because she attributes all the credit for everything that is good to God.

Mother Mary is so easy to access. She is, however, a being of the spiritual world rather than the material world. So you will need to use your spiritual senses to perceive her, not your physical ones. Yes, some people actually see her with their physical eyes, but most see her with their spiritual eyes or feel her with their spiritual perceptions. One way to develop a sense of what it feels like when she is present is to compare her presence to the presence of Jesus. You must tune in to the subtlety of the spiritual realm. That means you must get very still and notice the slightest of changes in what you are feeling and perceiving in and around you.

Mother Mary infinitely hopes for every human to be changed and come back to God. She never gives up on anyone. She prays for us all night and all day. She is not interested in rules, only in the application of God's love through her to suffering people. She knows that if they will only allow her, she can heal them of their pain and lift them out of their sorrow. Mary's actions in our lives provide amazing miracles of all kinds. The most amazing ones are often in the realm of how she can and does change our entire attitudes and feelings about things. In doing so, she makes adjustments of how we feel about something or someone which are permanent and deep. In my experience they are more amazing than physical healings are.

There are very simple ways to invoke her help with a situation you feel stuck with: First, get on your knees. Why? It places you in a position of humility. If you also open your arms and lift your hands, you have placed your body in such a way that it will help induce the right attitude which states that you are aware that you need help, and you are open to receive it. Reach up in mind and heart and contact Mother Mary. The best attitude to have in this is just know that if you reach up to her, you will contact her because she is right there and never refuses anyone's request for help. Next, ask her to come into the situation for which you are imploring her help and change it. Then let it go. Thank her in advance because you can know she will do it. Then go about your business while staying open to a new thought, attitude or understanding of the situation to show up in your mind and heart. The answer often comes within half an hour or so, sometimes not until later that day, or when you go to sleep. But if you are open, you will without fail receive a whole new understanding and attitude regarding the situation, which will change everything about it for you.

Mary works within us to adjust the attitudes, perceptions and feelings that cause us pain, sorrow and anxiety. She heals the brokenhearted and leads them to peace. She is the greatest healing power and most accessible of anyone known to humankind. She never judges us, is never critical, and always receives us as her children, her beloved ones, on whom she has compassion and whom she wants to lead back into God's peace. The only way you will come to know her is to begin working with her in these ways. Thinking about her, theorizing about her, debating her existence or her ability to help all waste your time. You can do those if you want, but you might consider simply opening to her help and trying it out. Soon you will have no doubts as to her reality. If you are worried about whether it is right to be contacting her, ask her to show you that, too. You can also ask her to introduce you to her son as there is nothing she would rather do.

I do not wish to say more about her because this is not an intellectual topic. If you want to experience whether she is real or how she heals, just try her, and then be still and receive her gifts. You will be blessed beyond all imagining. In her love be blessed.

CHAPTER ELEVEN

Devotion:
The Royal Path to God Within

Thou hast made us for thyself, O Lord,
and our hearts are restless until they find their rest in thee.

~ Saint Augustine

In order to begin to work with the inner world, or what you might call the "spiritual world," you will need to develop various skills. You will need to practice letting go of thoughts and emotions, which create noise and blockages in your inner or spiritual world. You will need to learn to concentrate and focus. And you will need to develop your inner sight and other spiritual senses so you can begin to perceive the otherwise "unseen" world of spirit and start to work within it. With diligent work and the help of a spiritual teacher you will learn to use your mind to bring about changes in the material world. Without the ability to concentrate and see the other side of existence that lies in the spiritual world, you will not be able to do any spiritual or inner work at all.

Though all these things I have mentioned are important, none of them will get you into a direct relationship with God within your being without one essential thing: Love. The Apostle Paul, in Corinthians 1: 13[2], wrote:

> Though I speak in the tongues of mortals and of angels, but do not have love, I am a noisy gong or a clanging cymbal. And if I have prophetic powers, and understand all mysteries and knowledge, and if I have all faith, so as to remove mountains, but do not have love, I am nothing. If I give away all my possessions, and if I hand over my body to be burned, but do not have love, I gain nothing.
>
> Love is patient; love is kind; love is not envious or boastful or arrogant or rude. It does not insist on its own way; it is not irritable or resentful; it does not rejoice in wrongdoing, but rejoices in the truth. It bears all things, believes all things, hopes all things, endures all things.
>
> Love never ends. But as for prophesies, they will come to an end; as for tongues, they will cease; as for knowledge, it will come to an end. For we know only in part, and we prophesy in part; but when the complete comes, the partial will come to an end. When I was a child, I spoke like a child, I thought like a child, I reasoned like a child; when I became an adult, I put an end to childish ways. For now we see in a mirror, dimly, but then we will see face-to-face. Now I know only in part; then I will know fully, even as I have been fully known. And now faith, hope, and love abide, these three; and the greatest of these is love.

The school of spiritual development through which I teach is under the direction of the Masters Jesus and Mother Mary. The

---

[2] Victor R. Gold, Thomas L. Hoyt, Jr., Sharon H. Ringe et. al. *The New Testament and Psalms: An Inclusive Version*, Oxford: Oxford University Press, 1995

path they brought us and which they direct is the path of love. It is through their immense love for all of humankind and for each of us individually that we have the teachings and the initiations and sacraments that bring us back to God. It is only through the development in us of love for God and for other people that we can become full God-beings. Yes, we emphasize working with light and filling with light, because light is the visible presence of God. But the action of that presence is love. We learn to take in light and become filled with light, so that we can then pour forth love – love for God and for all of God's creatures. As Paul said in the scripture, "Without love you are nothing." Nothing. Do you really get that? Nothing. All these teachings and fancy spiritual attainments you work for are nothing without love.

How can you begin to allow this love to move through you? How can you come to love God, Jesus and Mary deeply? How can you come to love others and yourself in the way God loves you? Is this love something you can will yourself to feel? Jesus would have given himself up for crucifixion for just one of us to come to God. Mother Mary would have endured the torture she endured witnessing her son's agony for just one of us to become whole. How can you come to have that much love for God and your fellow humans? How can you come to love your brothers and sisters who walk beside you on this path, and those people who hate you and wish you harm, that deeply? What will you have to become to carry that much love in your heart?

You will have to become a Christian, which means "Christ-like," if you are to be profoundly filled with that deep of a love. And how did Jesus and Mary love those who were persecuting them? Before they served as they did on the earth they had come into an intimate love relationship with God that was so intense and present in them that they were transformed into embodied love itself. Secondly, through their relationship with

God, they saw people as God sees them. God sees a world full of frightened, hurt, sad and confused people, who need love so badly that they live in excruciating pain because they do not know that they are God-beings at their core. They do not know that in that core of their being lies the source of all love. The pathetic sadness of this situation, where people all over the world are starving for love while it lies right there within their own beings, compels God and God's servants, Jesus and Mary, to continue day and night working toward bringing all people into that love relationship that will fulfill all their needs.

The easiest way to begin to feel love for God is to learn how to be open to feel God's love for you. If you even feel a little bit of how much the God-Self loves you, you will inevitably begin to feel a great love for your God in return. The same goes for relating to Jesus and Mary. It is not easy to open to such incredible love. We have to first get over our resistance to it, which is often based on our sense of not being worthy of it or being afraid to be obligated by it. When we can simply allow ourselves to be loved by them, then we will begin to be able to feel love for them, too. Then we will start to learn to love others as they do.

To develop greater devotion for Jesus and Mary and, through them, develop a greater devotion for God, you can do a simple spiritual exercise. Sit in front of a picture of Jesus or Mary. While focusing on the picture, quiet your mind and heart and prepare to receive impressions and feelings. Then ask Jesus or Mary, "Jesus (or Mary), do you love me?" Be really still and open your heart to receive. After a bit, ask it again. Do this three times at one sitting. Do it each night for two weeks. Without fail, if you have opened yourself to the influx of their love, you will feel it. And as you do, you can begin to learn from it. Absorb it, explore how it moves in you, let it fill you and then look out at the world through the perspective of their love. Look at yourself through the perspective of their love. Begin to let that perspective become the perspective with which you go through life.

The devotion that will develop in you toward our great masters and toward God will start to pour through you. With it you will be able to, "bear all things, believe all things, hope all things, and endure all things," as the scripture says. With it you will become a force for good in this earth that can transform the darkness around you, as you cannot, at this time, imagine possible. And it all begins with your opening to receive and experience Jesus, Mary and God's love for you.

This great love is what I feel for each of you. This great love is what I wish for each of you to come to know. Bringing this great love to all people is what my mission on earth is about. I invite you to join us in this mission of love.

CHAPTER TWELVE

Living as Monks for God in the World of the Senses

A saint is a sinner who never gave up.

~ Yogananda

People who have little, if any, experience with contemporary mystics often have trouble understanding why some spiritually-inclined seekers tend to develop a very high level of commitment and involvement with their spiritual communities and teachers. After all, most who consider themselves faithful church, temple or synagogue attendees do not attend more than once a week. Why, they ask, do some seekers attend so many events at their spiritual centers and, even when at home, do daily practices and intensive introspection? Why are they seemingly obsessed with finding and clearing all conscious and unconscious issues that might keep them from God? It might seem to you that these people should be satisfied with being good people who believe in God and who are a part of a regular religious community like everyone else. You may even feel suspicious of any spiritual path that suggests people do more than only attend, but instead actually immerse one's self in an ever deeper spiritual life and inner growth.

Perhaps it will help you to understand the mystical spiritual path if you think of those practicing it as monks, though they often still live and work in the world. Monks are people who have decided to make their relationship with God of foremost importance in their lives. The commitment has two aspects to it: First, it is the daily practice of drawing ever closer to God within them. Once they come into that presence, they enter into it and begin the process of becoming one with it. This is a significant part of a mystic's daily practice, no matter whether they are being still in meditation and prayer or if they are active. The intention is to always stay tuned into God and always to grow deeper in that attunement.

The second aspect is that of service to God through service to others. When monks live in monasteries, they are mostly doing the monastery's form of work, whether that be farming, making various things that get sold to support the monastery or working to maintain the facilities. Their service to others is the very maintaining of that center of holiness in the cities of the earth. Through their frequent prayers and services they draw down much grace, mercy and light upon all the surrounding communities and their residents. Communities traditionally felt very blessed to have such monasteries amongst them, feeling them to be a source of safety and support for all the people for many miles around, as they called down light and peace upon all people. In fact, many towns were built up around monasteries, holding that space as the spiritual center of the city.

Today, a growing but small number of people are embracing living more like monks than like most people in the world. Some of us are combining living as members of society in a work-a-day world with the depth, purity and commitment of the lives of monks. Most ordinary people of the Western world do not care much about God. And of those who do care, only very few incorporate their spiritual life into daily life, other than maybe offering up a prayer when they are scared or in need of help. Many actively state that it is wrong to make God more important than family in one's life. This occurs even though the scriptures of Christianity, which purportedly is the main religion of the Western world, state that God must come first in one's heart, mind, soul and life. Therefore, many people consider the very fact that some of us take the teachings of Jesus seriously very strange or even aberrant behavior. So what might motivate a person to live in such a different way than most people would think of as desirable?

The vast majority of people live in the world of the five physical senses. They primarily care about their bodies, and what makes those bodies feel good. Their second highest priority is to feel good emotionally and to experience contact with the world that provides them with emotional rewards. That often means seeking out who and what flatters them and gives them rewards that make them feel that they are special and therefore important. Their lives are so empty of meaning that most have to constantly grab for something new and better in order not to get depressed, which has made the anti-depressant industry an increasingly booming business. They are hurt and do not know how to heal, and their lives are at various levels of meaninglessness. When a new baby is born into the family, or when a new romance is entered into, things brighten up for a while. Too often those children or romances are latched onto as the be-all and end-all of their future happiness. When the baby becomes a toddler throwing tantrums, when the romances are never quite fulfilling over the long-term, people no longer know what to do. Often they then enter into more and more dysfunctional and depraved behaviors in an attempt to make things more exciting and more alive. These people may take on addictions, sexual excursions into what is weird and distorted, or sports and hobbies that become the most important aspect of their lives. In all these ways people try to not feel the desperate loneliness and emptiness of their existence on earth.

There is a voice within every one of us that calls out to us. Some people are more willing than others to hear the voice from within that is telling them there is more – this voice calls us into a life of the spirit. In Western culture many hear that voice and in response dabble in various forms of alternative spirituality. There are so many various forms that it has actually become common for people to take innumerable different classes in everything from developing your psychic skills, to yoga, to exotic meditational practices and numerous other forms of fringe spirituality. I call them "fringe" because most practices barely scratch the surface of relating to a spiritual life and therefore may be fascinating but do not actually transform anyone. When a serious spiritual group comes along that can offer the full service package of the way to God and the way to healing all your wounds and transforming your long-held problem areas, most people don't know what to make of it. If you, as a seeker, come to me inquiring about the spiritual path I know and teach, I will tell you that if you want this, it will take some serious work and a changing of your orientation from being dedicated to those outer sense experiences to dedication toward the inner path to God. Achieving the desired goal of oneness with God will take more than going to church once a week. It will take a complete overhaul of your ways of being in the world. That does not mean that you will need to give over what is already of God and functioning well within you, but you will need to give over all that is not of God, so it can be healed, transformed and raised up. When you go to the dry cleaner and you want all your clothes cleaned, you have to hand all of your clothes over to be put through the cleaning process. If you want to withhold some choice items so that the cleaners don't scrutinize them and see where the spots are that need more intensive treatment and might need to go through the cleaning process more than once, then the cleaner won't be able to return to you an entire clean set of clothes.

Likewise, if you want all of you cleaned and made whole, you will need to be willing to hand all of yourself over to the teachers you choose because real teachers are the servants of the great cleaner of souls. If you don't give them all of yourself to clean, then they can't help you become completely whole. We know from experience that when people attend classes and services at our Centers of Light they get drawn closer to God and are inspired and lifted up for a day or two. But then they cannot hold it any longer and once again get lost in the world. That is why we say if you really want to progress that you need to attend a class or a service every few days. We also know from experience and from Jesus' teachings that the sacraments work wonders inside of people, transforming them from the inside out, because they bypass the conscious mind and work in secret within your heart, mind and entire being. That is why we tell our students that they should really make coming to Sunday services a regular part of their lives if they want to move along toward God and toward healing in their entirety. We also know that if you do not do your own inner work, developing your spiritual skills and proving through your daily practices to God that you are serious and are willing to make the time and do the work, you will not move along as well. We also most clearly know from experience that, unless you allow someone to teach and guide you, you will move so slowly in your growth that you are bound to be disappointed when you reach the end of your life and look back and see how little you grew and changed.

We have developed the recommendations that we give new students beginning a spiritual path and what we stress as being essential to their growth based on these experiences with students. Some immediately see what we mean and posthaste go about re-structuring their lives around the goals they have decided to embrace. Others agree to do some aspects, while holding off on committing to other parts of the program for quite some time. Still others attend this and that, now and again, often then deciding as a result that we really don't deliver what we claim to offer because they aren't experiencing much. Or they may believe we have what we claim to offer but do not believe that they are capable of taking it all on. They often ask us whether it could be made easier for them.

When you ask us this, it is as if you were saying that you want to go to the top of Mount Everest with us because you want the feeling of accomplishment and success. You want to see the view and have the glory of attainment, but you don't want the difficulty of the climb or to have to carry your own pack. What do you imagine you are asking? Why should you have that experience of being on the peak if you are not willing to do the work to get there? We are metaphorically taking a group up to the peak of Mount Everest. We have made the hike ourselves under the guidance of our own teachers. We have led numerous other treks up that great mountain and have welcomed a number of people into that great joy. Some have, in fact, given up after having started the ascent. Others have given up at various other levels of the climb. Some even get to the top and then do not want to help any others get there. This is sad for us, but we accept that it is the way some people are. Our commitment is to keep leading treks up that mountain and to train others to be trail guides and leaders. Every time another person asks to be taught how to climb it and is led to the top, we and the angels rejoice and sing. Every time someone decides it is too much work and they had rather read about others who climb, there is sadness from all those who know the truth about the mountain and the climb.

Very few people even dream of making their way up the treacherous Mount Everest. Even fewer actually try, and of those not all succeed. So it is with the real path to God. Jesus said that the path to life is narrow and there are few who walk it. We are like monks in that we dedicate our lives to the attainment of oneness with God. People who think of doing this seriously are as few as the ones who think of climbing Mount Everest. And, as with the great mountain, even fewer people actually do it. In our order, we give our lives to this quest of entering into oneness with God while remaining in the world. We continue to hold jobs, some of us have marriages and raise families, some are in school and furthering our careers, and we do it all while placing God first in our lives, our hearts and our minds.

We who live like this are an anomaly among the monks and among the outsiders. The level of our dedication and the intensity of our practices is perhaps more understandable to you if you think of it in the context of monastic life. When a person enters a monastery, they are not expected to show up for all the family functions from then on. In fact, most monastic traditions allow their monks to see family only on a very limited basis. The monks are not expected to have social lives with people on the outside as they did before. Their families know that that is over, that the monk's new life is now with their fellow monks and priests, and that the events of their lives are centered around that which is spiritual and no longer around the family. So it is with us. When people get more serious about the spiritual path, they tend to prefer to be with those who are of similar mind and heart. It is the same in other aspects of life. If you are a dedicated consumer of alcohol, you generally would prefer to be with those who do and want the same, rather than with those who have no regard for this activity. If you love model airplanes, horse racing, or dancing, you would tend to spend most of your free time with those who do the same. You can share your common enthusiasm and practices and enjoy supporting each other's progress and successes along the way when you are with those of like mind.

On the spiritual path, we tend to find what used to be of interest and the people who used to seem entertaining are not so interesting or entertaining anymore. We don't tell people to avoid those who are not on a spiritual path; it is more that after some time, these people do not seem to be as interesting to the serious spiritual student. When the seeker wants to speak of what they are learning, people who are not of the same mind tend to be disinterested or do not appreciate it, and the seeker soon finds that sharing their spiritual growth with others ends up feeling bad. The seeker starts finding that the way they can share with the people who are doing the same inner work as they are is so deep and fulfilling that they want to be with them more. This, then, is how an ever deeper communing with the seeker's spiritual community comes about as they move along the path with us. To the world, we then seem increasingly strange in that we appreciate being with each other more than being with other people. If you understood the monastic model and our similarity to it, you might be able to grasp what we are doing a bit better.

But very few would understand why anyone would want to be a monk, so we warn spiritual aspirants not to expect to get much compassion from presenting that model, either.

To be in the world while not being of it is the directive Jesus gave us. We, who take these words of Jesus seriously, practice what he said with our whole beings. We decide not to participate in the mind of the world, that mind which worries and frets and tries to compete and gain through worldly means. We decide not to participate in the heart of the world, that heart, which envies and hates, fears and desires what belongs to others. We decide not to participate in the body consciousness of the world, that consciousness which lives at the mercy of the five senses and believes that our bodies are to be served and filled with whatever they demand.

Instead, we choose to live in the mind of God, that mind which knows it has power to create and chooses to create what is in accord with the will of God. We choose to live in the heart of God, that heart which is pure, loving and compassionate. We also choose to live in the body of God, knowing that our bodies are temples of God and are to be cared for but not indulged, disciplined and kept holy so that they can be pure vessels to contain God within them and manifest God into the world.

We of Jesus and Mary choose to live as monks while in the world. We choose to live in purity while walking amongst depravity. We choose to have hearts filled with love while surrounded with hatred. We choose to make God and our service to God everything while living among those who care nothing about God. We choose all the things of light and commit to shine this light in the darkness. We give our lives, our hearts, our minds, our bodies and our souls to God, as we joyfully live in fullness in the world. We give thanks for the great privilege and opportunity to do so. Blessings upon all of you who choose to live as monks while living in the world and as lights shining in darkness. Blessed be the way. Blessed those who walk it. Blessed those whom we can serve.

CHAPTER THIRTEEN

Your Way or the Way of Grace

Enough of phrases and conceits and metaphors!
I want burning, burning...

~ Rumi

Having the spiritual path your way means you can call all the shots. You don't have to submit to a teacher to be taught. You don't have to do anything you don't want to do. You can read some nice books and feel really spiritual. You can hang out with others with whom you have an agreement to pat each other on the back about how spiritual you all are. You can make sure you don't get too close to God because that might get uncomfortable. You can be politically correct and say that everyone's path is equally valid. You can incorporate established religions or leave them out, whichever makes you happy. And if you learn enough impressive spiritual lines that you can take on an air of holiness, people may begin to consider you a spiritual teacher and look up to you.

There is another way, which is the way of following a true path to God and being taught by real teachers. Within that true path, there is a way of living, a way of being raised up spiritually. We might call it the way of grace. This way of grace is very closely linked with Mother Mary, with her who was called "Full of Grace." What has Mary got to do with grace? How did she come to be full of grace, and why does it matter to us?

Mother Mary says in *The Poem of the Man-God*:

> I promised you that He would come and bring you His peace. Do you remember the peace you enjoyed at Christmas! When you saw Me with My Child? Then it was your time of peace. Now it is your time of pain. But you know by now, it is by means of pain that we achieve peace and every grace for ourselves and our neighbors. Jesus-Man became Jesus-God again, after the tremendous suffering of His Passion. He became Peace, once more. Peace from Heaven, from where He had come and from where He now pours out His peace for those who love Him in the world. But in the hours of His Passion, He, Peace of the world, was deprived of that peace. He would not have suffered if He had had it. And He had to suffer: and to suffer excruciatingly, to the very end.
>
> I, Mary, redeemed woman by means of My divine Maternity. But that was only the beginning of woman's redemption. By refusing a human marriage in accordance with My vow of virginity, I had rejected all lustful satisfactions, deserving thus grace from God. But it was not yet sufficient, because Eve's sin was a four-branched tree: pride, avarice, gluttony and lust. And all four were to be cut off, before making the roots of the tree sterile.
>
> By deeply humiliating Myself, I defeated pride.
>
> I abased Myself before everybody. I am not referring to My humility towards God. Such humility is due to the Most High by every creature. Even His Word had it.

It was necessary for Me, a woman, to have it. But have you ever considered what humiliation I had to suffer from men, without defending Myself in any way?

Even Joseph, who was a just man, had accused Me in his heart. The others, who were not just, had committed a sin of disparagement with regard to My condition, and the rumor of their words had come like a bitter wave to break up against My humanity. And they were the first of the infinite humiliations I was to suffer in My life as Mother of Jesus and of mankind. Humiliations of poverty, of a refugee, humiliations for reproaches of relatives and friends who, being unaware of the truth, judged Me a weak woman with regard to My behavior as a Mother towards Jesus, when He was a young man, humiliations during the three years of His public life, cruel humiliations in the hour of Calvary, humiliation in having to admit that I could not afford to buy a place and the perfumes for the burial of My Son.

I overcame the avarice of the First Parents renouncing My Creature before the time.

A mother never renounces her creature unless she is forced to. Whether her heart is asked to renounce her creature by her country or by the love of a spouse or even by God Himself, she will resent and struggle against the separation. It is natural. A son grows in our womb and the tie that links him to us can never be completely broken. Even if the umbilical cord is cut, there is a nerve that always remains: it departs from the mother's heart and is grafted into the son's heart: it is a spiritual nerve, more lively and sensitive than a physical one. And a mother feels it stretching even to exceedingly severe pangs if the love of God or of a creature or the need of country take her son away from her. And it breaks, tearing her heart, if death snatches her son from her.

And I renounced My son from the moment I had Him. I gave Him to God. I gave Him to you. I deprived Myself of the Fruit of My womb to make amends of Eve's theft of God's fruit.

I defeated gluttony, both of knowledge and of enjoyment, by agreeing to know only what God wanted me to know, without asking Myself or Him more than what I was told. I believed unquestioningly. I overcame the innate personal delight of enjoyment because I denied myself every sensual pleasure. I confined flesh, the instrument of Satan, together with Satan, under My heel and made of them a step to rise towards Heaven. Heaven! My aim. Where God was My only hunger. A hunger which is not gluttony, but a necessity blessed by God, Who wants us to crave for Him.

I defeated lust, which is gluttony carried to the extreme of greed. Because every unrestrained vice leads to a bigger vice. And Eve's gluttony, which was already blameworthy, led her to lust. It was no longer enough for her to enjoy pleasure by herself. She wanted to take her crime to a refined intensity and thus she became acquainted with lust and was a mistress of lust for her companion. I reversed the terms and instead of descending I have always ascended. Instead of causing other people to descend, I have always attracted them towards Heaven: of My honest companion, I made an angel.

Now that I possessed God and His infinite wealth with Him, I hastened to divest Myself of it saying: "Here I am: May Your will be done for Him and by Him." He is chaste who chastises not only his flesh but also his affections and thoughts. I had to be the Chaste One in order to annul the one who had been unchaste in her flesh, her heart and her mind. And I never abandoned My reservedness, not even by saying of My Son: "He is mine, I want Him," since He belonged only to Me on earth, as He belonged only to God in Heaven.

And yet all this was not sufficient to achieve for woman the peace lost by Eve. I obtained that for you at the foot of the cross when I saw Him dying, whom you saw being born. When I felt My bowels being torn apart by the cry of My dying Creature, I became void of all femininity. I was no longer flesh, but an angel. Mary, the Virgin Spouse of the Spirit, died at that moment. The Mother of Grace remained, Who gave you the Grace she generated from Her torture. The female reconsecrated "woman" by Me on Christmas night, achieved at the foot of the cross the means to become a creature of Heaven.

This I did for you, depriving Myself of all satisfactions, even of holy ones. And whereas you had been reduced by Eve to females not superior to the mates of animals, I made of you, if you only wish so, saints of God. I ascended for you. As I had done for Joseph, I lifted you higher up. The rock of Calvary is My Mount of Olives. From there I took My leap to carry to Heaven the re-sanctified soul of woman together with My flesh, now glorified because it had born the Word of God and had destroyed in Me the very last trace of Eve. It had destroyed the last root of that tree with four poisonous branches, a root stuck in the sensuality that had dragged mankind to fall and that will go on biting at your intestines until the end of time and to the last woman. From there, where I now shine in the ray of Love, I call you and I show you the Medicine to control yourselves: the Grace of my Lord and the Blood of My Son.

> And you, My voice, rest your soul in the light of this
> dawn of Jesus, to gain strength for the future crucifix-
> ions which will not be spared you, because we want
> you here and one comes here through pain, because
> we want you here and the higher one comes the more
> one has suffered to obtain Grace for the world. Go in
> peace. I am with you (Valtorta, 1, 142-145)

This passage is loaded with truths of the way of Mary, the way
of grace. Let us begin to decipher them by looking at the four-
branched tree that Mary said was Eve's sin. The first branch
was pride. Mary tells how she overcame pride by allowing herself to be humiliated in every way. Her humiliations came as
people did not know who she was and what her motives and
reasons were for all that she did. She said she never defended
herself. She took on overcoming pride for all humans, so as to
undo the sin of pride that Eve committed. Are you aware how
much pride runs through much of what you do, say, think and
feel? Have you looked enough at pride to even begin to recognize it in its many forms? Whenever you do, say, think or feel
something that at its core says you are better than or special
in any way, you are indulging in pride. Pride is a sin. Why? Because anything that separates you from God is a sin, and pride
does just that. It separates you by making you who is most
important and who is to be served and catered to.

Mother Mary told God that she was not interested in preserv-
ing her pride but was willing to accept every humiliation to
pay off the debt of Eve and to overcome pride for all people. If
she had simply stated that she was above pride without being
tested and pushed in every way, she would not have sealed that
healing truth into the earth. By actually doing it, she opened
the way for all of us to enter into the grace of overcoming our
pride and living in the love of God above all else.

Are you willing to allow yourself to be humiliated for God's
sake, and for the sake of overcoming your pride? Would you

have the guts to make a prayer that stated: "God, I accept every humiliation you want to send my way so that I may be free of pride?" That is an enormous prayer, and don't make it unless you mean it and feel ready to take on that transformation because it is almost guaranteed to be quite painful. Any time we are humiliated and our pride is hurt, it is painful. And yet, it is the way into heaven, where those who are pure in heart dwell.

The second branch of the tree that Mary overcame is avarice. The dictionary defines avarice as "an extreme desire to amass wealth." It comes from a root that relates to greed and desire. You may know that you have a desire to amass wealth, even if it is not extreme, or you may feel that this is not one of your temptations. Let us look at avarice as Mother Mary addressed it. She said it would have been avarice if she had claimed Jesus was hers, in any way. So from the moment of his conception, she never let herself want to have him fulfill any desire or need of her own. If you want to see where you have avarice in your heart, look to see where you want people or things or situations for yourself, to fulfill your needs or wants. Do you want a partner who will make you feel better, who will love just you, for whom you will be the most beloved? Then your heart is avaricious, and you know nothing of love. Do you want material things to fill a need in you for people's envy or respect, for their attention or love? Then you are avaricious.

There is a subtler form of avarice, too. Do you want spiritual gifts, initiations and ordinations for something you will get out of them? Do you want others to look up to you, to admire you? Do you want them to look to you as someone with spiritual knowing? Then you are committing the sin of avarice. Why is it a sin? It is a sin because it separates you from God who is the giver of those gifts. They are not given to you to fulfill a need in you or stroke your ego. They are given to you out of love and for you to use them to serve others and bring them into the love God gives you. If you are looking to amass spiritual gifts or powers then you are not walking the path of grace that Mother Mary brought us. You are continuing to walk the way of Eve. Remember, Eve wanted to be like God, and that was one reason she ate of the apple. She did not want to be transformed into the love of God, which would have been a good choice for her. She wanted the power of God, to be equal to God, to have knowledge for herself. That is how she was avaricious.

Mother Mary tells us in *The Poem of the Man-God* that the third branch of the tree of Eve is gluttony. Gluttony is defined as extreme intake of food and drink. It comes from the desire to take in more and more without any regard to how much of what foods are needed. Food is meant to give our bodies energy so that we can go out and work and affect our world in a positive way. A glutton worships food and drink as gods. Food and drink take on enormous importance instead of simply being the means to nourish our bodies. When we are gluttonous, no amount of food is ever enough. The same holds true if you want to consume more and more spiritual food, keeping it only for yourself and not letting the light and love you were given shine out into the world. It is as if you are stuffing your face with spiritual food and forgetting about everyone else. Mother Mary took this sin and overcame it through a beautiful purity. She states in the text that she overcame the gluttony of knowledge and enjoyment. To overcome gluttony of knowledge, she did not want to know more than what God wanted her to know on any subject, and she never asked herself or God the reasons for things, or for more information. She simply believed.

Can you imagine entering into such simplicity where you don't even want to know more than what you are told, and instead you simply believe and obey? Eve wanted to know everything, so Mother Mary asked to know nothing unless God wanted her to know. Many times she did not know how situations were going to work out. She did not know how Jesus was going to be born in Bethlehem, as he needed to be in order to fulfill the prophecy. She did not try to make it happen or to organize it. She left it to God. God arranged for the Roman census to be ordered at that time, which required everyone in the Roman Empire to go to the city of the head of household's birth. Joseph was from Bethlehem, so Mary and Joseph had to go there just in time for Jesus' birth. Mary did not know how Joseph was to find out about her pregnancy. She let God take care of it, in faith, though it was extremely painful for her to not share the news and to see Joseph doubt and suspect her. She did not know they would need to live in Egypt. In fact, God did not tell her but told Joseph instead, and she accepted it. Every step of the way she stayed in faith, without demanding to know. And as such, she defeated gluttony and opened the way for us to do so, too.

The fourth branch of Eve's tree is lust. Mother Mary states that lust is gluttony taken to an extreme. She describes how gluttony involves us alone indulging in excessive satisfaction of the desires of the flesh. Lust gets someone else involved, and drags another person downward, even if only in your mind. When you lust for someone you are dragging them down to indulge with you in animality. There is no love involved in lust, only extreme greed. You want not only your own satisfaction but you want someone else to help you attain it. When you do that in your mind to someone, you are wronging them by seeing them as nothing more than a body you can use, even if only in mind, and ignoring that they are a spirit made in the image of God. Mother Mary overcame lust by always ascending, always rising up to higher consciousness. Instead of trying to drag others down, she always lifted them up to heaven by seeing and helping grow the God within them and never focusing on their flesh.

We lust not only when we desire someone sexually but also when we want them to fulfill our gluttonous needs. When we use others as means to get our greedy needs met we are being lustful. When we want to drag others down to the low level of consciousness that we are indulging in, then we are lustful, too. When we want our spiritual teacher to desire us in a romantic or sexual way, we are then also being lustful. If you find yourself having such dreams or fantasies of your teacher, it means you don't want him or her to be on the level of consciousness they are on because that means you might have to transform, too.

If you can imagine him or her being of a lower human nature, then you have dragged him or her down to your level and can discount what they say and the fact that you need to transform. Whenever you lust, you make the satisfaction of your desires so important that even others should have to serve that god you created to meet your needs. As Mother Mary said, Eve went beyond the gluttony of indulging her own desires to getting Adam involved in indulging her pleasure; thus she became lustful.

Mother Mary overcame all temptation to want to have pleasure for herself or to have anyone else give her pleasure. She led all others heavenward, not downward, and thus overcame the sin of lust. Now she had the serpent and its servant, the flesh, crushed under her foot. In doing so, she opened the path of purity for all of us. However, having done all of that was not enough for her. Now that she had conquered all the sins of Eve, she still had to give her life in order to become the Mother of Grace. Having to watch Jesus be crucified at the hands of hateful humans and hear his dying breath inwardly killed Mary. She said that at that moment, Mary, the Virgin Spouse of the Holy Spirit died, and the Mother of Grace remained. She immediately turned around and gave that grace that was generated by her torture and her overcoming of all sin, for us – every one of us – that we might enter into a life of grace.

If you look at Eve's sins, you will see that each is a sin of the desire nature. Our desire nature, whether we are men or women, is a part of our feminine nature. Mary took on the work of redeeming the desire nature for all humans. Jesus once said that out of the heart come all manner of evils. It is our desire nature that pulls us down and away from God, and our desire nature that can bring us to God. Mary showed us how she overcame each of those temptations of the negative desires. Pride, avarice, gluttony and lust all come from the desire to take something for ourselves in a measure not given by God. In pride, we want people's admiration and to think of ourselves as better than others. In avarice, we want more than we need or have coming to us and want it all to ourselves. In gluttony, we want to consume everything excessively without having to give anything back from it. And in lust, we want to get others involved in fulfilling our base desires.

These things can be overcome within our hearts. This purification of the heart is required of all those who want to be close to God. We may feel some sorrow in the process of letting go of attachments we have clung to. Much self-discipline and vigilance will be needed to keep ourselves from succumbing to the temptation to fall back into old patterns. We have to give up the fear that we will no longer get what we need when we stop trying to grab it for ourselves. We need to come to live the truth that we need only God. As we do so we give over to God completely and we allow ourselves to be filled by God.

How do we become carriers of grace as Mother Mary was? We do that by first overcoming each of the four branches of the tree of Eve: Pride, avarice, gluttony and lust. As we overcome each one and that vice no longer is active in our hearts, a space is opened in its place that will become a channel of grace for ourselves and others. Mother Mary did one more thing to become the Mother of Grace: She died internally and completely, as completely as Jesus died on the cross. Her crucifixion was of her heart rather than of her body. Her suffering and inner death was as deep and complete and brought life and forgiveness to humankind as much as Jesus' death did. What was left was the Mother of Grace. We can only contemplate in awe what scale of sacrifice she took on. We can offer our lives and hope and pray that we may become that purified and belong that entirely to God that we could be used for the raising up of the planet as Jesus and Mary were able to be.

If you want to come close to God and become a channel of grace for others, I recommend that you ask Mother Mary to show you how you indulge in each of the four vices. To the extent that you truly want to see your vices they will be shown to you. Ask that you see the grosser as well as the subtler manifestations of each vice in your life. Focus on one at a time while you keep the others in mind and stay open to seeing them too. Spend a week or two looking to see each one. If you have a spiritual teacher, when you see each vice tell your teacher about it and begin to transform each vice into a virtue. This is not a fast and easy process but is one that is essential to your transformation. You will not be the one who then needs to bring the grace into each place you vacate in your heart; God is in charge of that. But know that it will happen. You will become a pure channel of grace to the extent that you give over your heart to the purity of Mary.

May each of you be blessed as you enter upon this path of grace, under the holy protection and guidance of our blessed Mother Mary. May her presence be strong within and around you, and may she always be an inspiration and a hope for you along the way.

CHAPTER FOURTEEN

Relaxing into God

Don't struggle and strive so, my child.
There is no race to complete, no point to prove,
no obstacle to conquer for you to win my love.
I have already given it to you.
I loved you before creation drew its first breath.
I dreamed you as I molded Adam from the mud.
I saw you wet from the womb. And I loved you then.

~ Mpho Tutu and Desmond Tutu,
from *Made for Goodness*

Perhaps you read the title of this chapter and felt disappoint-ed. You may have hoped for a chapter that sounded more ex-otic, maybe one about connecting to the spiritual world. You may feel like relaxation is such a beginner's issue and that you addressed it ages ago. Why am I not addressing something more befitting your place on the spiritual path? In truth, there is no matter of greater importance to your life in the spiritual world than the issue of relaxation. One of my Sufi teachers, when asked what he wished he had done differently after fifty years of spiritual study and work, said, "I wish I had paid more attention to relaxation."

Why did my teacher say this? What is it that he had seen later in life that he had overlooked earlier on? Let's begin with the *American Heritage Dictionary* definition of "to relax":

> To make lax or loose, as in *relax one's grip*. To make less severe or strict. To reduce in intensity; slacken. To relieve from effort or strain. To become less formal, aloof and tense.

It comes from the Latin meaning *re-loosen.* In physics, it refers to "the return or adjustment of a system to equilibrium following displacement or abrupt change." An odd root meaning is "to have drooping ears." So being relaxed is the opposite of being stressed, tight, intense, strained, formal, aloof and tense. It is about returning to a state of equilibrium we once had and lost. Relaxation is now addressed in medicine as a very important factor in preventing various diseases of the body, and it is spoken of in psychology as one of the essential ingredients to maintaining mental and emotional health. But why is it so important in our spiritual lives?

Relaxation is needed on all levels of our lives in order to enter into the spiritual world and obtain relationships with the beings in it. We need to relax physically, emotionally, mentally and spiritually. The physical body expresses what we are thinking and feeling and carries our attitude and way of relating to material objects and people. It is not possible to fully relax physically while holding attitudes, feelings and thoughts that are tense, strained, filled with effort, formality, severity or strictness. We can begin to relax the body and achieve a state of relaxation to some extent without fully adjusting the thinking, attitudes and emotions. But we cannot achieve deep relaxation without having loosened our grip on all levels of existence. If you want to open fully to God and to the spiritual world, you will only be able to do so to the extent you let go of all that you hold onto inside. Whether you hold onto an emotion, a thought or attitude, each part of you that is involved in holding those things is occupied, busy and not available to be filled with God's spirit, light and love.

Consider the attitudes that are inimical to entering a state of relaxation. One of the most prevalent ones is the state of mind of needing to get something done. The thought alone that you need to get any particular task done adds a sense of urgency to that action which makes your body, mind and heart go into a state of extra readiness and alertness. Your heart speeds up, your muscles tense and all the systems of your body prepare for action. This is a good state to be in when an action is about to be entered into that requires that type of energy. But we enter into that state many times when no such action is needed from our body. It is a state of trying to make a development happen, of looking to generate the energy for it to happen, of vigilance around it getting done the "right" way. You feel driven to get it done and to do it right. Or you think it is important that it be done the particular way you think it should be done. Over many years of frequently and unnecessarily entering into and staying in such a state, your heart, mind and body become habituated to it and learn to remain at some level of tension most of the time.

Another attitude that keeps us tense is one in which we are often or nearly always anxious that something negative is about to happening. The message we give our bodies, hearts and minds is that something could happen almost anytime, and we therefore need to remain prepared and in a state of watchful vigilance. Sometimes you may have that attitude because you are afraid for your physical safety, but often you are likely afraid of not doing something perfectly, of being told it is not good enough and of being rejected. When you live with this fear, you are in a stressed, un-relaxed state that affects you on all levels.

Another highly prevalent situation is one in which you may be afraid that there will not be enough. Not enough money is a very great concern for many people. Not enough love is an equally strong fear, or an even stronger one. Because of this fear, people who are caught in it feel they need to always be watchful and try to make sure they have enough and will have enough in the future. They stay in a state of tension, whether they currently have enough or not. The alarm keeps ringing inside their hearts and minds, keeping them in a constant state of high alert, which becomes the norm for their state of being.

The reason these states of tension matter to your spiritual life is that when you sit down and want to get still and go inside, you first need to get around the structure you have erected that supports the system of vigilance. If you try to go in without an awareness of it, you will find that it is hard to progress, to concentrate or relax. What is happening is that whatever amount of your consciousness is tied up in the maintenance of your tension, that part is doing the opposite of relaxing into God. You have two parts, each pulling you in an opposite direction. When you first begin your efforts to relax, the tension part is much stronger because it has many years of practice. The part that wants to be still and relax is a new baby and has very little practice and experience. You won't be able to stop doing something that you are not aware of doing. So the first step is to become conscious of how you tense up and what the causes of that tension are.

Once you are aware of how you hold tension, ask Mother Mary to show you what your attitude needs to be instead of the one you currently hold. Let her take you there and experience it. If you have to visit Mary several nights in a row, do so. Spend a half hour on your knees and let her open up the correct attitude for you. Once you understand what it needs to be, begin practicing it many times a day, not only when you begin meditation. Feel it move through you and change how you breathe, feel how your muscles relax, notice how your mind and heart feel. Then, in that new attitude, begin to live, move and carry yourself as a new being. It may take some time for you to change a lifelong habit of stressed attitudes and tension. Don't give up; it will come in time.

Now let's address the relaxation that is needed to go inside and draw near to God. When you first sit down to meditate, go immediately to your breath, observing it go in and out. Then relax your body, employing whatever methods you have learned from Mother Mary or have found that work for you to release tension. Often this will be some form of letting your consciousness open wide, while every cell in your body, mind and heart opens wide also. The visual sense you want to hold is one of having been inside something confined and now coming out into a wide-open space. All your tension and concerns fall away at the edge of your view as you open wide to peace, to stillness, to the all. Consciousness of your body will drop away as you become more aware of your spiritual body, which is less limited and feels more expansive. Now nothing in your physical body will distract you anymore.

As consciousness of the physical body evaporates, you can begin to turn inward, into the center of your being. You now seek to focus on drawing near to God inside of you. Notice what happens. Are you distracted by feelings that come up in you, or does your head start chatting away? What are those feelings or thoughts telling you? They may try to pull you into your outer consciousness and get you caught up in your usual ways. Or they may argue with you about how you have this problem or that issue that prevents you from getting still. Or they may try to get you to see how impressive those thoughts or feelings are. You need to learn not to get caught by any of those thoughts or feelings. If the feeling is a scared one, reassure it that nothing but good can come from drawing close to God. If these voices want to tell you all the issues they think you should first address before going to God, let them melt away and go in deeper anyhow. Remember: God is more important than your body, your feelings and your thoughts, no matter how impressive their calls for your attention seem to be.

When you come out of meditation, write in your notes what you got stuck on or what was happening with your body, feelings or thoughts. If you have a spiritual teacher, you may read these notes to the teacher, and he or she may be able to help you look at what is hanging you up. Often what you get stuck on will be some of the issues we addressed, regarding either needing to be in control, fears of something happening to you, or not getting enough love or care. So the roadblocks are good to see because they will show up what you need to address. Look at them and listen to them carefully. It is only through addressing these roadblocks that you will be able to learn how to let them go and enter more deeply into your inner being.

Relaxing into God means being glad to give over all control to God. You no longer exercise the right to decide whether you think you are good enough to approach God. You no longer let your body sensations, feelings or thoughts convince you that they need your attention more than you need to go to God. You no longer hold back because you are afraid that God might hurt you, control you, disrespect you or not love you. You relax into God. This is not a passive state. Many people think they are meditating when they sink into a good feeling, but God is beyond the good feelings. God matters more than your feelings. Can you believe that? To reach God, you will have to choose to make God most important within you and trust God completely, even without all the evidence you may want that God is trustworthy. Just think about it: you are demanding credentials from God, who feeds your every breath and keeps you and all of creation alive and thriving. That's just silly.

Relaxing into God is also something you can do all day. You do it by choosing to let go of your reasons to stay tense and by living in a new state of peace. Remember that God is all around you, in every breath you take and in the center of your being. You can relax now knowing how well you are protected and provided for and how wise God is in knowing what you need. This is what letting go and letting God is about. Practice such relaxation many times a day, learning to go deeper and deeper into it. Watch how you are breathing during the day and that will give you a good place to start. Watch what you are thinking and feeling; tuning into how your body feels. Then choose to relax again and again into God and into God's love. Nothing could feel more satisfying, nothing could be safer, and nothing could be better for you than such a life in God. May you be blessed as you learn to make a new pattern in your life of always relaxing into God.

CHAPTER FIFTEEN

Going Deeper

Deliver me from assuming that mercy is gentle.
Pressure me that I may grow more human,
  not through the lessening of my struggles,
  but through an expansion of them
  that will undamn me
  and unbury my gifts.

Deepen my hurt
  until I learn to share it
  and myself
  openly,
  and my needs honestly.

Sharpen my fears
  until I name them
  and release the power I have locked in them
  and they in me.

Accentuate my confusion
  until I shed those grandiose expectations
  that divert me from the small, glad gifts
  of the now and the here and the me.

Expose my shame where it shivers,
  crouched behind the curtains of propriety,
  until I can laugh at last

through my common frailties and failures,
laugh my way toward becoming whole.

Deliver me
 from just going through the motions
 and wasting everything I have
 which is today,
  a chance,
   a choice,
    my creativity,
     your call.

Let how much it all matters
pry me off dead center
so if I am moved inside
 to tears
  or sighs
   or screams
    or smiles
     or dreams,

They will be real
and I will be in touch with who I am
and who you are
and who my sisters and brothers are.

~ Ted Loder, *Guerrillas of Grace: Prayers for the Battle*

Spiritual teachers often use the words "going deeper" when speaking about a student's growth and development on the spiritual path. I have told many students that they need to work on going deeper, and I focus on bringing them deeper through exercises, blessings, teachings and prayer work. I get a sense that it is often not clear to many spiritual students what is meant by the term and why teachers emphasize this so much. So I will address this and clarify the importance, meaning and process by which you will find yourself deepening as you move along the way.

To strive to go deeper is important no matter where you are on the path. It applies to beginners as well as to priests. It also applies in all aspects of being and functioning: In your psyche, feelings, relating, understanding, searching and connecting. It applies to your relationships with yourself, with others and with God. Without striving, you cannot progress along the spiritual path. In contrast, with it, you can meet God face-to-face and come into holy union with God. Now you may want to know "How do I grow that striving and when will I arrive there?"

When you first come across a spiritual school, which is real and deep, it will likely not take long before you feel that something is going on that is deeper than what you have encountered in life before. You may not use those words. You might instead think of it being more real than what you have felt in churches or other spiritual schools. Or you may find it mysterious, intriguing, moving, feeling it drawing you inward and making you want to follow. You may find that what occurs in the Sunday services, in classes and when you are given blessings makes you consider God, Jesus and Mary in a new and different way and urges you look at yourself, your feelings, thoughts and actions, motivating you to live your life with more care and thoughtfulness. The vivid descriptions of experiences that new students have when coming upon a real spiritual path stem from the fact that these teachings and practices go deeply into the reality of who we are, who God is, and how to come into a totally real and life-changing relationship with God.

Specifically, what does it mean to go deeper in the various aspects of our lives as human beings? Let us begin by considering our relationships with other people. Most human relationships are extremely shallow. Our first relationships are with those who were responsible for caring for us, usually our parents or a parent. The parent, or parent substitute, took care of your body at least enough to get you here today alive.

They may or may not have done a good job of caring for your intellectual, social, emotional and spiritual development. But parents who actually set a child free to become anything they want to be are quite rare. When, in addition, they teach the children to find their purpose on earth, that God is central to knowing and fulfilling that purpose, and they set them free to find God in whatever form they are called to, those parents are of a very rare caliber.

Most often what happens in that early relationship with your parents is that they attempt to make you what they want you to be without any reference to your soul's needs or desires, not paying attention to who you really are. Some did even less than that and just considered you a bother and a burden, at least part of the time. Many of your parents let out their own anger and frustration on you, using you as a recipient for their physical or emotional outbursts and perhaps also for their sexual desires. All the while, you experienced them as the ones who were supposed to love and care for you and who instead never even saw you for who you were; or when they got glimpses of your essential "you-ness," they did not respect or support it. You did not see them as people either because they were to you a role that they were supposed to fulfill, not people to get to know.

The failings of your parents' and others' care for you formed in you feelings of unmet needs, fears, mistrusts and sadnesses. Those feelings carried over into how you related to everyone else from then on. They formed your ideas of what you wanted from people in your life and how much you would let them in. The way you relate to others, based on your needs and fears from childhood, is not a deep way to relate. If you find you are needy towards others and always want more love and attention, then you are relating from the shallowness of unconscious wounding from childhood. If you are demanding of others, or if you do not let them come close enough to connect with you, then you are also staying in the shallow waters of your past hurts and fears. But fear not, this can be healed, and there are simple ways you can go deeper in relating to others.

A deep relationship with other people will be based in your understanding of yourself. You will have to enter into knowing yourself on all levels to be able to connect with another person in a deep way. What you are carrying from your childhood and from previous life experiences will have to be examined, seen and understood. Then it will need to be healed before you are able to come out of relating from your wounds enough to truly see and connect with another person. In the meantime, however, as you are getting to know yourself and beginning to heal your wounds, a deeper way to relate to others comes from the consciousness you are currently carrying. Sharing with others who are in a similar place on this journey of healing the past helps you begin to see how the same process manifests differently in different people. As you open up difficult and vulnerable feelings and experiences you have kept secret out of shame, you open them up and allow them to heal. As you listen with love and compassion to others' processes of healing, that healing energy touches you, too. This process of relating more deeply to others entails opening up to yourself and to others the places in you that are so hurt. That pain and the process of recovery from it is what all humans share, only manifested in different ways.

You now may want to know what it will mean to go deeper in how you relate to yourself. It will certainly involve the work I already mentioned in going deeper with other people. When you come to understand how your childhood and adult life experiences formed and affected you, you are at the beginning. But more is involved; you will have to come to an entirely new understanding of yourself that is built on qualities that are really you and not qualities and expressions that you have taken on from your environment. This involves looking at your likes and dislikes, where they come from and how you define yourself as a result of them. It means looking at your opinions and points of view with discriminating eyes and heart, seeing which are truly expressions of you as a soul and which ones you have taken on this life. What you will find is that the great majority of these things will not stand up to scrutiny as being true expressions of your soul. Most will be understood, when you look with your new consciousness, as being unimportant and frivolous. It does not mean that you need to be completely without preferences or opinions; it simply means that you need not take them so seriously. You will need to know that they are fun and mean nothing except that you have found them as expressions for this life and that you can drop them whenever necessary.

Going deeper in knowing yourself will also require a deep exploration into why you do what you do and think what you think. Many adults are still acting out a way of being that they adopted as teenagers or even earlier in their lives. It was how they felt they needed to be at the time to get the love and caring they wanted from those around them; or it was how they protected themselves from more pain. They were necessary coping mechanisms at the time. But now, years later, many people are still using the same adaptations that they learned as a child.

Some of you worry and express fears and weakness, hoping to get cared for and loved. Many of you want to be the very best girls and boys you can be, so that you will get approval and love and not have to hear any correction or what might feel like deadly criticism. Some of you act tough and like nothing can hurt you or get to you, or like you don't have to do what anybody tells you to do, still being rebellious and independent, often blocking out love as much as you block out anyone being able to help you. Very often people use combinations of these ways of expressing at different times. After some time, you will begin to see and understand yourself objectively. You did need those mechanisms to get through vulnerable and difficult years in your life, but now they only get in the way of you becoming yourself and finding your way to God. This cannot be done in a deep, thorough and time-efficient way without the help of a spiritual teacher. This means you need to let your teachers help you.

This brings us to the next way in which you need to go deeper: How you work with your spiritual teachers. In different spiritual schools, the steps and processes vary. When a student in my spiritual school begins preparing for baptism, this marks the start of the path for them. This involves doing an entire life retrospection and telling your teachers about it, which, for most, feels deeper than you have ever let anyone see into your life, your heart and your mind. Yet this is just the beginning. It can take quite a while before students realize how they could be using the time they get with their teachers in a way that will help them move along the path the fastest. Initially, students often only tell about what is going on in their lives and what they are worried about. They share about some of the neat spiritual things that are happening with them. Some people don't understand how important it is to do the exercises they are given to do every day and to write the notes about them precisely as they are instructed to do. For many students, this pattern takes months to establish. As long as your teachers still have to work with you to get that going, they cannot even start to go into the deeper realms with you. So the first few months are spent getting students to do the exercises as told, reporting on them well, and establishing within themselves the fact that they can trust their teachers. After you share with your teachers several very private and shameful things and you experience their compassion and help toward you in healing those wounds, you start to truly trust them. You start to get powerful results from the exercises, and you begin to establish some discipline in your personal spiritual practices. You attend classes and services at the spiritual center regularly. Your teachers will continue guiding you as you find your way and establish these practices in your life; as you grow and blossom, they will have supported you through all the changes.

Once students have established their practices and become regular with them, we can lead them deeper into truly placing God at the center of their lives. By this point a student will have had some experiences and gained enough understanding of God that they will state they want to begin to live their lives according to God's will instead of their own. However, much happens before the student is ready for this. They have come to understand that God really loves them and wants what is best for them and will never hurt them. They must have come to know that God also wants what is best for everyone around them. They must humbly recognize how limited their own ability to make the right decisions is and how they do not know what is right for them and those they love. They must also have come to trust their teachers enough to have them help them come to know God's will for them. And they have to be ready to do exactly as God tells them to and not just take God's guidance as another opinion they will consider.

When this happens in a student, we can then begin to help them find the answers from the "Still Small Voice" within. Sometimes, we help them get that guidance before they have actually reached this point because something important was coming up in their lives and they seemed willing to follow God's direction. But it is a quite different place when people are ready to begin to look for that direction and follow it in all the different aspects of their lives. Then they have begun to truly want God to be the God of their personal world and they want to know God's direction. Somewhere along this time in a student's life they have often also come to hold enough light in their bodies that they can be brought into the initiation of the illumination. This initiation is for many the first introduction to the reality of a world and a way of being that is not of the earth. For some, it is a dramatic introduction, and for some it is more of a gradual, gentle opening to that world. Nothing is the same afterwards, if one really accepts the invitation to begin to live in that light that is given at the illumination. Suddenly, one begins to understand what one has previously heard spoken about and taught in a whole new way.

Within the reality of the spiritual world, all the perceptions of what one's life has been up until that time and what it is now begins to change. One begins to get glimpses of how God sees us and how God sees things in the world. One begins to get a bit of a sense of how the heaven worlds work and what we are here on earth for. With this awakening usually comes a much deeper longing to know and serve God and an awe and great gratitude for what God has given us. Now a student will start to see him or herself more as a potential part of God's plan for the earth. The inner guidances they now want to ask are often bigger in scope. And because they increasingly trust God and have a greater longing for God to come into their life more completely, they start to get in better contact with the God-Self within. In this way, their ability to get guidance begins to improve. This is when a student may feel the need to let the priest know that they would like to be a servant of the Most High through the school they are in, in whatever capacity that might be.

The deepening is not isolated only to your spiritual life. In fact, everything else in your life will have been getting deeper too. If you are married, you will have gone through all kinds of changes in how you relate to your spouse and how you understand yourself and your spouse in that relationship. If you are single, you will have metamorphosed your ideas of what you want in a partner and in a friend and in what you seek from family life. You will have learned so much from your brothers and sisters in your spiritual community, and you will have deepened in your relationship with your teachers. After two years of individual training in our school, some people may be invited into minister training if they have expressed a desire to do so and their teacher sees that calling in their hearts and a readiness in them. Some students will instead let their teacher know that they would like to take vows in a sub-order, the Order of Mercy, through which they will serve the elderly and their communities.

Most students who choose to enter into minister training are quite shocked by the difference of the teachings given when they start that training. Now, instead of everything being centered around your own processes, trials and tribulations, you are told that God will take care of you. You, in turn, need to start thinking about and caring about other people more. The training is no longer about how you need to allow things to come into you and transform you, but rather how you need to let them come in and transform others through you. You begin to be taught how to bring these wonderful experiences that have brought you thus far to other people. The level at which you are worked with will also be quite different from how you previously experienced your training. Previously, your teachers had been for the most part simply supportive of your processes. Now we really begin to work with you to deepen and purify your being on all levels.

At this point, we no longer expect to have to cover the most basic points with you. We instead expect you to have those down. These would include your knowing the value and importance of attending regular spiritual services and classes and that you would naturally and very willingly place attendance at those above all other priorities, except when guided to do otherwise. We would expect you to have worked through a lot of things and be ready to spend most of your training on how to help other people. That does not mean we think you will be perfect now, only that you will be ready to give. Most of you will sometime during your minister training come up against something or several things that feel huge to you and have to be transformed. We will help you and support you when you are going through these things. When you do get clear from them, you will be ready to be an ordained minister.

As a vowed brother/sister in the Order of Mercy you will be taking on responsibility as a servant of God through serving others both in and out of your spiritual community. You will also have had to reach a point of purity and humility in which you can be happy to be of service without needing it to be about you. As an ordained minister, the same is required. In addition, both types of servants of God need to continue going ever deeper in their reaching toward God and letting God enter them and their lives in every way. Neither minister nor vowed brothers/sisters are now meant to only focus outwardly. They must be doing the inner work of filling ever more with light and taking that light into the world in whatever they are given to do. And they must keep drawing closer to the God-Self at the center of their beings. Once you start to focus on helping others by understanding what they need and letting God move through you to guide and heal them, your life becomes so much richer in so many ways. You will begin to feel that you have found your place on earth and the supreme joy of fitting into your place in God's great plan to bring love, light and healing to all.

This may seem like the ultimate of what can be a reality for our work on this planet. If you are not yet there, it is, in fact about all one could even try to imagine becoming. And yet I tell you there is still much more. As deacon-ministers continue to go ever deeper into their willingness to turn over all of their life to God and their understanding of how to do this, both outwardly and in their feelings and thoughts, they will naturally want to know God better so that they can have more of a direct relationship with God. They will want God to show them how to do everything, not just the big things according to God's will. As this longing grows, they will use the light that is growing ever stronger in them to look deeper and deeper towards the center of their being. When they have purified themselves of other desires and longed and sought after God for some time, God may then tell the master teachers that this soul should be introduced to God face-to-face. This is when we bring deacon-ministers into the initiation of self-realization. The veil is re-moved, which had previously kept them from seeing God, and they are introduced to the one who made them and who has loved them for all these years, who has been longing to come into this relationship of love for which God created all humans.

You must be thinking: How could one possibly go deeper than that? Yes, it is true; there is nothing deeper than God. But self-realization is an initiation, which means it is the beginning of a face-to-face relationship with God. In it, the veil is removed and you then have direct access to God to get to know God and to get direct guidance from God. But it will still be up to you to do those things. You will not know God simply from having seen God. The truth is you will understand much more about everything, especially who you are, but now you will have to seek out this God you have just met, often and deeply. You must have many, many interactions with it in order to get to know it. Once you have truly come to rely on it, trusting and going to it for all your needs, you may be called to be a priest. Deacon-ministers commit their whole lives to serving God. Priests vow the rest of their existence to serve. Why would anyone want to do that?

To want to serve as a priest, one would have to have come to a place of seeing nothing else one could do on earth to be as great an honor and joy. It doesn't feel like a sacrifice then but a commitment to doing what you want to do most. With that commitment comes the blessing of God bringing you back to opportunities to serve each life. As a priest, you no longer have the luxury of taking longer periods of time to work on your own stuff, however, you continue to grow. When you are first ordained you are once again just beginning a new level of service. It will take some time to fully take that on. In the priest ordination, the new priest says that he or she agrees to continue his or her training and in fact, they continue growing, deepening and training for the rest of their lives. We work with the priests intensively to support their work with students and to help them continue to go deeper into God and the service of God. This is a level of functioning that is not possible to imagine unless you are there. I can only tell you that the deepening continues for all eternity, until one is like Jesus and Mary and is all God.

I hope this has helped to give you some understanding of what we mean by "going deeper." Some of you may have thought it applied only to understanding your own motives and inner psychological and emotional workings. Some others may have thought it applied to feeling things deeper down in your body. Yet others may have thought it applies to knowing the higher levels of the teachings. I tell you that it does apply to all those, but most of all it applies to the depth you will go into God. When you are living within God at the center of your being and that God is now living throughout you, then you are living deeply. Up until then, you still need to go deeper. Every day. Every meditation. Every prayer. Every sacrament. Every initiation. Every ordination. Every breath. Every life.

Mystical Roses of Peace

CHAPTER SIXTEEN

Living in Christian Community

What happens when your soul begins to awaken in this world
to our deep need to love and serve the Friend?
Oh, the Beloved will send you wonderful, wild companions!

~ Hafiz

You may live in a Christian community, or you may only attend events at one, or you may have never been around a real one before. Many people have found themselves quite drawn to finding a dynamic and honest Christian community. Once they find one, they often discover that they are living, as in "finding their life" within the Christian community that they are worshipping and growing with. If this is your situation, you will likely over time get a growing feeling for the greater community that your spiritual center is a part of, whether that is an order, a denomination or other spiritual organization. When you stretch your understanding and heart to where you can embrace the larger group of affiliated communities and centers of worship, you will feel a strong connection with the extended group of ministers and members of all the centers that are a part of the Christian community you are living and "finding your life" within. A strong sister and brotherhood forms.

Some of you may have fears and resistance about agreeing to be taught by a spiritual teacher and some others of you may have more fear and resistance about membership in a spiritual community. Just as you cannot grow much without letting someone teach you, so your growth will also be limited if you do not immerse yourself in the life of your spiritual community. Humans were not created to be alone but rather to be social. Much of what we have to learn comes to us through relationships with others. Our relationships present us with some of our greatest challenges in life. Whether you are currently in close relationships or you want to be, or you are afraid about being in one, close relationships are never a neutral issue for human beings. Spiritual teachers frequently have to focus again and again on their students' close relationships, helping them work out the problem areas and heal from past wounds suffered from being in relationships that hurt. And most of you who are not currently in an intimate relationship tend to need your teachers' help in periodically revisiting your hopes and fears around the future possibilities of such a relationship.

We are, in fact, meant to share our thoughts and feelings and life experiences with others and we are meant to receive theirs in return. There are a few exceptions to this: Sometimes a person is told by the God-Self in inner guidance, or by Jesus or Mary, that they are to share only with them, or with them and their teacher. That may be the case for a limited time, or on a particular subject matter, or in some rare instances for their entire life. You should not assume you are to do this unless you have gotten this in inner guidance and your teacher has confirmed it. That guidance will not often be given because people need to learn and grow from their relationships with others. It is through these relationships that you can expand your perspective and can get a sense of how others see you. We are often quite blind to how we come across to others and we truly need other people's feedback to come to know ourselves and to be able to make conscious choices about what we want our impact on others to be.

To learn from other people's mistakes is a wonderful gift. When you have the opportunity to be around others who are sharing their successes and failures, you have a chance to learn exponentially more than what you can learn in one lifetime by yourself. To not have to make each mistake yourself in order to be able to learn a lesson is a great advantage. In a conscious spiritual community, you have a chance to see and hear your peers and from those who are ahead of you on the spiritual path in addition from those who are less far along than you are. Many times I have heard students tell how much they have learned from what other students were sharing. If, however, you do all the listening in order to learn from others without giving of your own experiences for others to benefit from then, in a way, you are stealing from them. Often the experiences, thoughts and feelings that are most difficult for us to say are the ones that are most important for others to hear. Jesus says that we must lay down our lives for our brothers and sisters. An important way to lay down your life is to share those things that you are struggling with or have struggled with and what you have learned from those struggles.

Some of you also have a tendency to say too much. When you are over-sharing, you are often entirely focused on yourself rather than on the other person or the people listening, thus not noticing or even caring that what you are saying is not useful or maybe even harmful or offensive to them. You simply want to get it out to feel better and you have not checked to see whether this is an appropriate forum in which to do so. Another reason you may over-share is that you may want a certain kind of response from people. You may want them to admire you, or you may want sympathy. Either way it is all about you, not about them or about you in relationship to them. Sometimes it is, in fact, appropriate and necessary to ask someone to listen to you so you can express some feelings or because you need to process a troubling issue. In such a case you need to find the right person. If you choose to talk with a peer in the community make sure that they are up for it and also that it is not always you bending their ear but that you also do that for them when they need someone to listen to them.

A great and wonderful gift that can come from living in spiritual community is that we can learn that the person we have always strived to be or tried to pretend to be, so as to be liked, is actually not very appreciated by other people. And, if your fellow community members have some consciousness, as many will who are on a serious spiritual path, they will see right through it. This may have been your greatest fear, that people will see through your façade, that you will be unmasked and then rejected. Or you may have projected out a façade, which is not for the purpose of being liked, but so that you might be feared enough that others will not dare to hurt you. Or you have projected the "tough guy" act to make people think they can't hurt you, because it would hurt you more if they knew they had gotten to you. Some of you have the good girl or good boy story running your life. It would be very scary for anyone to see you as not being so very good. This is a wound and is based in your belief that you have to be very, very good in order to be liked.

We are usually the last ones to know that others can see right through our games. Most of us put up with each other's façades quite graciously, understanding that people need to do some strange things in order to be comfortable around others. At some point during your life in spiritual communities, however, you may find out that people would actually prefer that you just be yourself. The 'yourself' that you are so embarrassed about and that you feel so desperately is inadequate and therefore must be hidden is in reality much more pleasing to others than the façade you display. It is so refreshing for people to be who and where they are, to not have to puff themselves up or tear themselves down to try and please everyone. This opportunity to become more of who you are and find out that people don't reject you is an enormous benefit of truly allowing yourself to immerse in your community of spirit. You will find that people are actually quite compassionate and understanding when you are who you are. It is a joy to see a person's soul shining through, and that can only come about when you give up trying to be someone other than who you are.

Real Christian communities that are committed to being conscious and holding great integrity are likely different than other communities you may have been a part of. These communities consider it entirely acceptable to join while you are still very imperfect. In fact, everyone in such a community would expect you to have some fairly big issues that are going to be hard for you to face. Everyone would be expecting you to be acting somewhat strange while you are going through big changes. People also will be accepting that you may at first be very clumsy when using your new skills. Some of you have to learn to be more assertive in saying what you feel. While you are first learning, you may come across as an elephant in a china shop. It takes time to learn how to do that the right way. Some of you have to learn to share less of what you feel. You also may come across clumsy at first, either saying too much or clamming up and saying nothing. Some of you need to learn to connect more with others, some of you less. Some need to speak up more in classes, some less. Each of you has to go through awkward changes, and I often watch your spiritual brothers and sisters bear with you as you learn to function in a new way. Often it is very deeply moving to watch you care for each other when one of you is having a hard time and trying to learn how to be comfortable being yourself.

Some of you have days or even weeks where you can do little else but cry. The community will let you know they love you and are there if you need to talk. But in the meantime they will be quite willing to let you cry as much and as long as you need to. Some of you go through periods when you feel you cannot accept other people's love, and you have rejected them and been mean to them. I often watch other members be patient with those lost in loneliness while rejecting love, and I watch them let you know they will be there when you are ready. Some of you feel compelled to stay away from the community for a while. I have heard others tell you they miss you and are hoping you will come around more. I hear many of you who are in spiritual communities telling me how you pray for each other. I hear you saying that you heard that someone is having a hard time with this or that, and you have held them in your prayers all week.

Do you have any idea what a treasure you have in being able to have such a community of brothers and sisters? I know it doesn't always feel all-wonderful or that obviously supportive, but in these conscious Christian communities, if something needs to be addressed to make you feel more respected or loved, it is encouraged that you bring it up. Because here every person wants to become more aware of how they can be more loving and more effective in their relationships with others. So even if it is painful, everyone here wants to be told the truth if they are hurting or offending another person.

What an amazing treasure such honesty and integrity is in a community! In a community that has teachers, you also have the benefit that most people are working with a teacher. That means that there are unbiased mediators to help whenever differences arise that need to be addressed. The Apostle Paul said that if you have something against another person in your community, you should go to them and tell them. If they still do not hear, you should take another person along to try to help. If that does not work, bring in a church elder. And if they still don't listen, stay away from them. In conscious spiritual communities, we have an opportunity to do precisely that with each other. And no one who is working with a teacher will choose to simply ignore an issue because everyone pursuing spiritual growth is dedicated to addressing issues as they come up. So we are blessed beyond all measure to have spiritual peers who are committed to growth.

What about finding a life partner within your community? You may already be married or you may have a partner who is also on the same spiritual path as you are. Or you may have a partner who is at this time not choosing to participate with your spiritual community or may not choose to do any spiritual development work. I know this can be a great sadness if your partner does not want to join you in your pursuit of spiritual growth and development. To you I say: Be patient, he or she may yet come. Don't judge or push them. You can pray for them, but you must give them the same respect and freedom that God gives us all, which allows us to choose to lead a spiritual life or choose not to. God does not harass us or love us less if we do not love God. God simply continues to love us. You must do the same with your partner if he or she does not choose your spiritual path or any spiritual path. Pray that your partner will feel God moving in his or her heart and that they may wish to respond to God. Pray that you will be a loving inspiration to your partner, not a nagging or judging pain. Then let the issue go. We teach that when you make a prayer, you must then let it go and leave it to God to manifest. You must do the same with your partner. Keep him or her in your prayers and in your love, but leave it up to God and them what their relationship with God will be.

Most of you who are single hold hopes of finding a person with whom you can share your spiritual and day-to-day life. Often there are many single folks in conscious spiritual communities and very few form into couples. Have you wondered why that is? In virtually any other group of people, many singles will try out having an intimate relationship with another or even several people in the group within a year or two's time. In a truly conscious Christian community, that will not be the case. Is it because such communities somehow manage to draw the most unattractive people on earth, or do they magically find many people who never feel attracted to any other community members? Clearly this is not the case.

You may first come to a deep inner spiritual path and community wanting nothing more than to find your ideal partner, have the perfect romance and then get married. It is a dream most humans hold in common. You may also hope to have children. I am often told from spiritual students that they see that in recent years they have put that dream above their search for relationship with God. Once you start working with a teacher and getting to know yourself better, you also increasingly begin to recognize how much work you need to do to become the kind of person who would be able to give real love to another person. And some of you have realized that you will not likely attract a partner who is emotionally and psychologically healthier than you are. So if you have many unhealed parts in you, you will most likely attract someone with many wounds, too. Initially you might really enjoy sharing the pain of your wounds and might feel so supported by the other, so understood. But after a while you will probably find that you are both stuck in relating to each other from your wounds. That tends to get old really fast, then somehow it doesn't seem wonderful or romantic any longer.

The reason that few couples form in spiritual communities during the early years of a student's involvement is that members are busy working on getting clear and healing their wounds. As a new student you are also trying to take heroic steps toward loving God above all, even more than you desire a mate, even more than your hopes for children, above everything! You may find that you enter into a much deeper trust that God will give you the right person whose soul is matched to yours, and this will happen when the time is right. The further you get on a spiritual path, the more obvious it often becomes that to start a relationship with someone who is not walking the same path with you is very likely going to be accompanied by many difficulties. It is not impossible, but wouldn't it be sad not to share with your partner what has become most important in your life? When you are already partnered with someone when you start on a path to God and they do not join you, then you make the best of the situation. But if you have a choice, would you really want to choose to add the complication of not sharing a spiritual path to your relationship?

When any of my spiritual students come to me and say they really would like to find their life partner, after talking with them for a while I may ask inner guidance with them to find out God's perspective. Does God see this as being the right time for this student to be open to finding a partner? If the answer is no, then the student needs to keep their partnering energies inside them and not reach out, not even shop with their minds or eyes for a partner. At some later time we can ask again. If the answer is yes, then I will talk with them about possibly beginning to explore connecting with someone. From that point on, every step of the way is done by first seeking inner guidance. If the prospective partner is not on this path, getting guidance will be only for the one on the path, which is not an impossible situation, but more difficult than if both prospective partners can seek inner guidance together. If you are both on this path, then coming to know each other is also a part of your spiritual unfolding and therefore can be very powerful and dynamic.

The fantasy that most folks have about having a partner who is on the same spiritual path as they are is that the two would then share all their spiritual experiences with each other. In reality, that is not what works best in couples. It is wonderful when your partner shares your dedication to God, Jesus and Mary and your involvement in your spiritual community.

It also helps when they understand that you need time to do your inner work and how much time needs to be given to your spiritual growth. It is great to come together to a state of being where you both trust God and you learn to get inner guidance and you both commit to base your lives on the guidance you get from the God within you. Life gets very exciting, as you never know what wonderful new opportunities lie ahead. To serve God together, giving an example of a dedicated Christian family is wonderful, too.

What isn't part of a shared spiritual life is talking with each other very much about your inner experiences and growth. This is where most people's fantasy of such a union goes wrong. If a couple shares their inner experiences with each other, they are often either placing themselves or the partner in a teaching function. Either you are trying to teach them something or you are awaiting their observations and input on your experience so that they can teach you something. Neither of you are in any position to be teaching each other. Your agreement is to be each other's partner, as two equals, not as one great wise one teaching the other inferior one. That kind of relating would never allow you to truly be partners, as equals. The other problem that will frequently arise from sharing your spiritual experiences is that you will compare and to some extent compete with each other. As each experience is shared, there will tend to be some thoughts regarding whether you yourself have had similar experiences, or whether yours are better or worse than your partner's. If yours are better, in your humble estimation, do you then assume you have something over your partner, spiritually? Or if you perceive your experiences to be less impressive than your partner's, do you decide that he or she is truly a great spiritual being and you are dirt? Do you see the problems that will arise from such sharing? This is why we tell the couples we work with to please refrain from sharing such experiences with each other.

Those of you who have children and who bring them to functions at your spiritual community centers are allowing your children to have an experience of Christian community, as well. They will feel how much love and meaningful relating people in your spiritual center share. They will also have opportunities to learn to relate better to the adults and to the other children. As the priests and teachers observe your children and you with them, they can sometimes point things out to you about your parenting that you had not noticed or questioned before that can make a big difference in your family's life. And your children have the privilege of growing up knowing that there are real priests and teachers and that there are whole communities of people dedicated to serving God above all else. What a gift to them!

We have not yet spoken of a most essential relationship, which is present in these Christian communities. It is the relationship of each student with his or her teacher. Students will grow the fastest if they really open up and keep nothing hidden from their teachers. They also need to allow themselves to be taught. If a student continues with their life much as they did before and only gives final reports to their teacher of issues and events happening with them, their transformation will likely take quite a while. If, however, they honestly tell their teacher what is going on in them and talk with the teacher while they are in the middle of some crisis, and they listen and accept what is being told to them, they can grow at an amazing speed.

In our order, every person who is either a student or a deacon or a priest, is in a working relationship with a teacher. Therefore everyone is connected to the master teachers either directly or through those teaching them. If one of our students begins training to be deacon, he or she begins being taught by an advanced priest. If a student takes vows in the Order of Mercy and becomes a brother or sister in it, they are provided with supervision by the priests directing them. Even priests keep talking with the master teachers and receiving help and instruction for their personal continued growth and for their teaching and ministering to students. In this way, the master teachers are actually a part of everyone's growth and development. We are keenly aware of this, and we know of the progress each student in our order is making through what their teachers tell us or from what we observe directly or while praying for all of them each night. This is the role of the guru in Eastern practices. We oversee the growth and development not only of the order itself, but of everyone being taught through it. These are threads of connectedness and support that go out to each person as they strive to deepen in their connection with God, Jesus and Mary and overcome the things that have been holding them back from becoming whole. We feel so much love and respect for each member, because we know what courage it takes to put one's foot on this path when the world is often quite opposed to it. And we thank every person who joins us in this work and trusts us to teach and love them enough to get healed, whole and in touch with God.

Now I would be greatly remiss if I did not address another relationship, the most important relationship of all that operates in our order and forms the backbone of any real mystical Christian community. Without it there would be no orders, we would not be teaching anyone, and no mystical Christian schools would exist. What I am referring to is that Jesus and Mary are the high priests of all true Christian communities. It is they who called our order into being through revelation. It is they who called me into the service of God and into my function as a master teacher. It is they who oversee the teachers of our order and who guide us and teach us and tell us what to do. As I described how we, the teachers, in our order are connected to each member of our order, so are Mary and Jesus connected to each one. They are connected to each one even more so because it is their order and they personally oversee the growth of every student and minister in it. They bring each of us all the love and light and guidance we can stand. They protect us from ourselves and from others when we are in danger. It is their love that makes it possible for any of us to be transformed, and their love brings us to God. Only through them do we see the face of God, in ourselves and in each other. We would be nothing without them.

What you receive through a deep and true mystical Christian community is everything your soul has longed for and more. Through the teachings, the relationships and the love of Jesus and Mary which you can find in such a community, your thirst and longing for God, for community, for growth and for deepening in a life of love will be quenched. If you have such a community, appreciate it, make full use of it, and love those around you who are becoming your family in God. Open to drink in the blessings that are yours through your community in Christ. And give God thanks for loving you so much to give you Jesus and Mary, teachers to guide you, teachings to live and learn by, and brothers and sisters with whom you can share the path to God.

CHAPTER SEVENTEEN

Giving of Yourself

In order to give us a precise and clear example of humility
in the perfection of love, [our Lord] took a towel
and washed his disciples' feet. So what about you,
living entirely on your own,
how will you ever discover such humility?
Whose feet will you wash? Whom will you care for?

~ Basil the Great

Most people want to feel that they contribute at least in some small way. People want to feel like their being on the earth makes a difference, at least to a few individuals. And many people dream of being able to contribute something that would make a difference to a lot of people. There are, of course, the many people who live quite selfishly only for themselves. These only wish to acquire for themselves, and often they give only to be recognized by others. There are also many people who are between the two camps, thinking they are contributing to others and convincing others that they are while doing so for entirely selfish reasons. Before I begin addressing giving of yourself, I want you to first examine if you are, in fact, one of the people who wants to make a difference on the earth. Do you actually want to have a positive impact? If so, how have you imagined doing that?

There are the overt, obvious ways that people can make a difference, and there are more subtle ways. Overt ways include openly doing good deeds and making changes that will have a lasting impact. These include social reform or service, charity works for the indigent and many other ways of helping. Then there are those who contribute in the field of healing, which can be of the body, mind, heart and/or soul. There are many different ways of contributing in those areas, too. One can work in any of the modalities of Western or alternative medicine and healthcare. One can give various kinds of counseling and therapies to address concerns and illnesses of the heart and mind. And much is given through these avenues to try to help in the care of the soul. In addition, there are all the ways one can make a difference whenever we are with people, not necessarily through the helping professions.

Is everyone who "helps" actually giving of themselves? And is there a right and wrong way to do that? If you want to give of yourself, you will need to be able to get out of your own way; you will have to learn to not care about yourself and focus on the other person. You will need to see a person's needs and not what you want them to need. You need to be willing to inconvenience yourself and also know how to do so without feeling like a martyr. You need to know and be willing to love in the way that is best for the other person, even when they don't want you to do what is best for them. You have to love them enough to discern when to forge ahead into territory within their hearts without their invitation and when not to.

How do we move from being quite unable to discern the needs of others to being able to see those needs and give to them in the right way? No one can traverse this path without first coming to know oneself and allowing themselves to be helped and taught by a teacher. Why can't we be helpful without knowing ourselves? In fact, we could be quite nice and giving in many ways without having done much inner work. Many of the people who help in charitable ways have done virtually no inner work. Outwardly, this can be fine. If the work they are doing is primarily in the outer world, they may, in fact, contribute a lot. But if their work includes dealing with the thinking, feeling and spirits of other people, they will soon run into difficulties if they do not know themselves. Even the nature buffs run into such trouble, though what they are championing may be trees or wildlife. They often become angry and judgmental people who spew large amounts of emotional pollution into the atmosphere while arguing against environmental pollution. They can become self-righteous and hateful of all those who do not see things the way they do and live according to the standards they hold to be right. The negativity they then exude has a more deleterious effect on the planet than the habits of the others that they are working to change. Thus their lack of inner work in identifying the sources of their anger and transforming those, including their lack of insight into how judgmental and self-righteous they are being, directly keeps them from being of help.

I will give you another example. Say you see your form of service as working with the poor. If you have not done your own inner work and you have not examined your motivations and needs, you might well be promoting the financially disabled to always stay that way. If you like your role of being "the one who has" versus "the one who does do not have" because you feel important or "good," then you will not see what they actually need. The issue of wanting to be good deserves serious examination. Do you have that desire to feel like you are good, or do you desire to have others see you as good? What are you getting out of feeling you are good or from having others believe you are? When you engage in charitable work to feel you are good or to be seen as good, you are, in fact, serving yourself above all. This will quite clearly affect the energy that will come across to those whom you are supposed to be serving and will close your sight to being able to see and give what is needed. Instead, this work will be about you and for you.

I trust you can now see why you will need to do the work to become clear and healed of your own wounds in order to even begin to give to others in a way that will be best for them. Once you do that work, and once you allow yourself to be shown your blind spots, you will be able to move to the next step toward becoming one of the beings on earth who give themselves into service. Now, what might that next step be? You will need to begin to see other people and really know what they need. In order to be able to have such sight and knowledge, you will have to become aware of yourself and know yourself. When you have allowed yourself to be taught and have experienced how a teacher has helped you, you will have a sense of how that can be done. You won't have the experience of how to do it yet, but you will have experienced love flowing to you from a teacher and how that teacher brought you far beyond where you could have gone by yourself.

Seeing what another person needs involves being able to sense their long-term potential, the steps that will get them there, and what they need to do now. Then you need to determine how much they are willing to be helped and how far they want to go. If you are working with someone who does not want help, you need to be able to have the strength and respect for their right to choose not to live more fully for now and let them go. Then you can find others who are more willing to use the help you have to give. They may also only go a short distance, and you will once again feel sadness that you cannot help more. You will need to allow that person to make the choice not to go farther at this time. Having the ability to see what people need and how far they can go, in addition to being able to know how healed and happy they could be are all attributes the teacher holds. However, having to accept how few actually want to do what it takes is painful to the one watching. Jesus said, "Oh, Jerusalem, Jerusalem, how many times did I want to gather you to me as a hen gathers her chicks under her wings, and you would not let me."

Once you have prepared yourself to give, you will need to have the love flowing through you that will enable you to withstand all the rejection and failure you will encounter once you try to help. That love is quite different than what most human love is. It is much more like God's love. God loves us whether we acknowledge and listen to God or not. God loves us even if we hate God and even if we work against what is good. That is because God does not allow any energy other than love to flow from God to all the creatures on earth, and God never tires of loving us over all the years of our many lives. God always looks to the part of us that holds light and God sustains the thought that this part will, in time, want to come back to God. When we want to help others, we cannot expect to get acknowledged for that help. Sometimes people will be grateful, other times they will not; they may even turn against us after we helped them. Remember what people did to Jesus after he fed them, healed them, taught them and raised them from the dead? They cried out in a frenzy of hatred for his crucifixion. Why would it be different for us? Do you believe you are better than him, and therefore you will be more acknowledged for what you do for others? You need to look for your reward for your good work to come from a source that is not an earthly one. You will need to learn to tap into God and be satisfied with God's approval of your work, when humans are not giving you any such approval.

Where can you learn to love that way? You will need to have opened to being loved that way yourself, either by God or by people. When you have received selfless and limitless love from others, then you will have an experience of what that is like and how amazingly healing it is. When you have allowed this divine love to flow into you and lift you up into ecstatic oneness with it, you will feel so grateful that you will want to give such love to others, too. You will understand their resistance to and fear to allowing you to give to them and love them, because you will remember having resisted and felt fear, too. You will understand their attachment to holding onto their pain and fears, their anger and shame, because you were once just like them. You will strengthen by accepting and not being too discouraged by their rejection and sometimes even hatred of you, because you remember Jesus and most of the saints and givers of all times having received similar treatment. In such times, you will know to turn to God for all your needs and all the support and approval you need. You will run to Jesus and into the arms of Mother Mary, and there you will be revived and once again charged up and ready to go out into the world and love again.

Giving of yourself means that you give everything you have that can be of help to another person. That may be time, insight, compassion, material help, or support. It could be guidance, assistance with their life tasks, hope, courage and confidence. You may be able to give someone a vision of how things can work out or what they can be or do, which are things that they might not be able to hold for themselves. You may be able to impress upon them that you do, in fact, know that there is life beyond where they are, and that God is love, when they cannot know that yet for themselves. In whatever way they need it and can accept it, giving of yourself means you will help them to move along their road in life and in spirit.

In the order in which I serve, all the priests and deacons have allowed themselves to be loved and helped in these various ways I have described, by their teachers. They have all come through their places and times of darkness, have accepted guidance, and they have learned how to traverse to the other side of that trouble. They have all trusted and wanted to change so that they could help others. They stepped out beyond where they could see ground under their feet and opened their hearts to let love in, even when that was the scariest thing they could imagine doing. Few challenges are as scary as allowing yourself to be truly loved. But you will never be able to give of yourself and contribute to others if you do not let yourself be loved first. When you open to being loved you clear the channel of love inside of you so that love can flow through you to others. The more you allow yourself to feel that love, the more love will naturally flow through you. Everyone in the whole world is longing for love. Everyone is dying of a lack of love. This love can take many forms, but it is always love. So you can only be a contributor of good in the world if you have learned to love by allowing yourself to be loved first.

When you allow a spiritual teacher to teach you, you may initially be astonished to experience what clear love feels like. It is not what the world teaches us that love is. It is not demanding, controlling, or sappy sweet. It is not conditional, where you are loved if you fulfill the requirements or are good. It won't always feel nice or easy, either. When a teacher loves you, they will give you what you need, which at the moment may not feel like what you want. They see the bigger picture for you and see what is in the way of your getting there. It is their job, out of love for you, to show you those erroneous beliefs and habits you have that are keeping you from becoming whole and being steeped in God's love. You may feel stinging when you are told that someone else actually sees your issues and shortcomings. You may feel challenged when they affirm that you do have a choice and can change those things in your life. You may not want to hear them tell you that you will not be able to enter into peace and joy without addressing and transforming these issues. And yet, would it be loving of them to hide the truth from you and thereby prevent you from healing and becoming whole? Would it be kind for them to keep the experience of the bliss of divine love to themselves and side with you in your belief that you cannot do anything to escape from your condition? That would not be love, though it might feel like they are nicer people than when they point out what is embarrassing and hurtful.

Do you, after hearing all this, then truly want to give of yourself? If so, I recommend you start by giving your spiritual teachers permission to give to you. That means you let them know that you want them to speak truth to you, even if it is not pleasant. And you will trust that they are not being mean or hurtful for the sake of being hurtful. Allow them to love you, sometimes by giving you applications of salve to your wounds and sometimes by lancing them open to allow the air to dry them out and the sunshine to heal them. Real spiritual teachers have no motives other than to give to you the great peace that they have come to know and to bring you into living in the phenomenal experience of knowing God's love for you as they have come to know God's love for them. We teach because we know the way. We love because we have been loved. We lance wounds because we know they need to be cleared of the infected puss that fills them if you are to become whole again. We pour into those open wounds healing balms of love and light because we know you need those, too. We know sometimes you can't take any more of our love, and you feel you need to reject us and hate us for a while. We don't hold that against you. We will keep loving you, and when you return, we will work with you again toward wholeness and light unless you tell us not to. Open now to what is coming your way, you who wish to be givers of light, life and love. And someday you may be able to join us as bringers of these great gifts to others who are lost and in pain; and we will joyfully work side by side with you as we heal the brokenhearted, bring liberty to the captives and set the prisoners free. May the blessings of Jesus and Mary be with you as you open to love.

CHAPTER EIGHTEEN

The Order of Christ Sophia: How This New Religious Movement Came into Being

When we say, "I take refuge in the Buddha,"
we should also understand that
"the Buddha takes refuge in me,"
because without the second part the first part is not complete.
The Buddha needs us for awakening, understanding,
and love to be real things and not just concepts.
They must be real things that have real effects on life.
Whenever I say, "I take refuge in the Buddha,"
I hear "the Buddha takes refuge in me."

~ Thich Nhat Hanh, *Being Peace*

I am often asked how this order, which I co-founded, came into being. What would possess a person (so people ask me, usually fairly respectfully) to decide to start a mystical spiritual order? When I have told the story of how I came to found the Order of Christ Sophia with Father Peter Bowes, numerous people have asked me to make this history available in writing so that they might review it and share it with others who ask similar questions. The following is therefore the story of the events and developments that preceded the formation of the

Order of Christ Sophia and how its unique function and mission came about.

To get a true sense of this order's roots, we need to begin 2,000 years ago when Jesus Christ and Mother Mary were living on earth. At the beginning of Jesus' ministry, he invited twelve men to follow him and learn everything he had to teach them. These men immediately left their families and professions and began a three-year period of intensive training during which they traveled and lived with Jesus, learning from him, listening to his teachings, watching his healings, and living with him day in and day out. After three intense years of such training with him, he deemed them ready to be of service and to represent and teach others all that he had given them.

Though they were still far from perfect, Jesus blessed them into being his priests and ministers and left them to carry his love and his healing power into the entire world. Jesus did not teach only those twelve but had an additional group of followers that he had also healed in body, mind, heart and soul and who were deeply committed and transformed through their time with Jesus. This group was made up of women and men, and many of them proved to be as equally faithful and courageously loyal to Jesus as the apostles were. This group of loyal disciples made up much of the leadership of the early church, under the direction and guidance of the twelve apostles. Mother Mary was at the center of this group of apostles and disciples; and her influence and guidance lasted not only throughout Jesus' life but also for years following Jesus' ascension and even to this current time.

The early church was led by the apostles, who trained and ordained ministers, sending them out into all the known world to tell people about Jesus and Mary, teaching all that they had learned and passing on all the blessings they had been given. They healed the sick and taught the great truths of spiritual life, light and love. They also taught how through Jesus and

Mary we could become completely transformed to be as they are: Beings of light who are full of life and living embodiments of love. The early Christians were unimaginably persecuted, just as Jesus had been. They were considered a destructive cult and Jesus was seen as a deranged cult leader. The practices and beliefs they held were decried as heretical by mainstream Judaism. Much strife and division came between the new Christians and their family members and friends when they decided to join the early Christian communities. Often they were disowned by their families and portrayed as crazy and under some evil influence due to their choosing to commit to what was considered a cult. They were hunted down, thrown to the lions or otherwise brutally tortured and killed by the Romans, with the agreement of the Jews. However much they were persecuted, they grew ever greater in numbers, in dedication and in strength.

Tens of thousands of people heard the truth in what the disciples were saying and felt the love of God coming through them, and they gave up everything and joined the communities of Christians. They joined in ever greater numbers, even though joining meant virtually certain torture and death. They lived together and shared much of what they owned, and they took every opportunity they had to learn from the more experienced apostles and disciples. They learned how to enter into the blessed state of knowing Jesus and Mary in spirit and coming into union with God who dwells within each one. The spiritual light grew so powerfully within them that at times others could hardly look at them without shielding their eyes. They chose to follow Jesus' teachings above all other considerations in their lives. This choice, so misunderstood and hated by the people of the world, brought them into direct experience and knowledge of God and the spiritual world. This is where Jesus always proclaimed his kingdom was – in this direct experience. They became the great blessed ones of God, while they continued to be hated, maligned and persecuted by humans.

In the fourth century A.D., the Emperor Constantine declared Christianity to be the official religion of his empire and began forcing people to be Christians by threat of punishment or death. After such a long period of persecution one would think that this new development would have been a blessing; and in some ways it was. But it also contributed to a new kind of church, which grew to be largely made up of very insincere Christians who had little commitment and only practiced in a superficial way. The contrast between this kind of Christian community and the ones during the times of persecution was enormous.

The church now became an ever-greater political institution mixed with religious teachings. As one might expect, the corruption within this establishment grew and proliferated. Some people were still deeply dedicated to having fully committed lives as Jesus taught, allowing the power of what was possible through the mystical light of Christ and through Jesus and Mary's love to transform them completely. But most people now related to Christianity as part of their social and family agreements, more than having it as the central and most important part of their lives.

Those who wanted a deeper knowledge and experience of God often joined monasteries. But even the monasteries were full of people who were there for the wrong reasons, not out of love for God. During these early centuries the church was sorting out what it was going to pass on as the teachings of Jesus and what it was going to eliminate from the teachings and declare to be heresy. There was a vast divergence between the teachings that various sources claimed came from Jesus. In fact, the twelve apostles had spread out, preached and taught in many different places, as did the many disciples that followed. Each had their own understandings of what Jesus taught and what it all meant and how it should be practiced. For example, the Apostle Thomas went to Egypt and there founded the Gnostic Church. The Gospel of Thomas has portions that seem very in-line with the teachings of the four New Testament Gospels but also has portions that are radically different. Even though he had been one of the twelve apostles, the church decided to declare Thomas' teachings and the Gnostic Church heretical, the practice of which could be punishable by death. They did the same with many other versions of Jesus' teachings, as they sought to put together something they believed was coherent and would be best or easiest to teach and promulgate.

One teaching that was eliminated during this time was the teaching of Sophia, Wisdom, as the feminine counterpart to Logos, the Christ. Up until the 4th century A.D. an essential aspect of the teachings of Sophia, this feminine counterpart of the Christ, was that God was both female and male, and also neither. Mother Mary also held an elevated position within the early church. Then during one crucial debate between two archbishops at the first great Council of the Church in Nicaea in 325 A.D., it was decided that Sophia was very much like Christ and therefore could be eliminated from the teachings entirely. As such, in one fell swoop the divine feminine was wiped out of Christian teachings. It was also decided that reincarnation, which had previously been taught by most Jewish scholars of the pharisaical sects and some of those carrying forward the teachings of Jesus, was not beneficial for the church. It, too, was eliminated from all future teachings. This elimination of various early teachings was so thorough that most Christians today do not even know that these doctrines were once included in some of the early Christian teachings.

As the church had the sanction of the governments in Europe, it became increasingly focused on power and wealth and decreasingly interested in spirituality and the kingdom of heaven, which had been the entire focus of Jesus' teachings. In the 13th century, a young man named Francis who lived in Assisi, Italy, felt called to a very simple life after returning from fighting for the Crusades. He wanted nothing to do with the family business, which he was supposed to take over. He did not want to be a part of how the church practiced religion, which was steeped in politics, money and dead beliefs. He declared that he simply wanted to live as Jesus and his apostles did, dedicated to finding the reality of God within his own experience and giving his whole life over to what he felt was his calling. His father was furious at the choice his son was making. Francis told his father that he no longer needed him to be his father because from now on he had only God as his father. He left his family and began to gather other young men around him who saw in Francis a dedication and spiritual light and life that they also wanted. A spiritual order was formed, made up of those who took vows to follow Francis as their spiritual teacher and guide, to obey his directions, to be humble and to give their lives over in poverty into the service of God. Soon thereafter, a young woman named Clare asked Francis to allow her to form a women's order that would be established under the same guidelines. In it, women would take the same vows as the men did but would live monastically instead of out in the world.

Numerous men and women from Assisi left their families, which were often affluent, to become utterly poverty stricken, begging for their food and rejoicing in their newfound life in God. They considered the other men and women who were vowed to this life in God to be their new family, their brothers and sisters in Christ, led by Francis and Clare. Most of the families of these young men and women who were left by their sons and daughters in order to join these orders were horrified and asked the church to intervene. Clare's family tried to forcibly bring her back to their home and make her marry. They said that Francis and Clare were exerting some kind of control over their children to make them lose their minds and their family loyalties. They said that their sons and daughters were talking all kinds of nonsense, speaking as they never had before about their new family being in the order and their old lives as being over, now that they had tasted of this new life of spirit and love, of devotion and sacrament. They were convinced their children must be under some evil influence, or why else would they leave their families and their previous lives in order to be part of this crazy movement? As Francis and his students walked the streets, singing and begging, they were often yelled and spit at and accused of many bad things.

Francis considered it an honor to be allowed to be defiled as Jesus was. His love for Jesus was so immense that he spent hours each day in contemplation and prayer. Jesus told Francis in a vision at the beginning of Francis' mission that he wanted Francis to rebuild his church. Francis initially did this by physically rebuilding a run-down chapel near Assisi. In the end, history attributes the credit to Francis for rebuilding the whole Roman Catholic Church at large. He did this by launching it into a new era of monasticism that was deeply devotional and mystical in its practices and life. This brought even the pope to his knees before Francis. Francis changed the church; this simple little man who loved God above all else, who chose the spiritual life above all material life, who chose God as his father/mother, and chose those who were vowed in his order as his brothers and sisters. Francis remains the favorite saint and example for many Christians today.

The years went by and Francis' purifying influence on the church wore off as the church once again descended into a cycle of enormous corruption and greed. Martin Luther was a monastic priest and scholar within the Roman Catholic Church early in the 16th century. As he saw the corruption growing, he eventually decided that he had to address the church and its corruption. He became the initiator of the reformation, in the wake of which many people left the Roman Church and declared their right to have their own faiths and develop their own ways of relating to God. Though the corruption and manipulation of the Roman Catholic Church needed to be rejected, some aspects of Catholicism were also lost, which many people, now Protestant, wish had been kept. One of those is the veneration of Mother Mary. The Protestant churches, by leaving Mother Mary behind, no longer had any feminine representation within their beliefs and practices. One result of this was that they often became very intellectual and theological, losing the devotional aspects that so many find in Mother Mary. Another loss was that most Protestant denominations let go of many of the sacraments of the Roman Catholic Church, keeping only baptism, marriage and a form of communion that is commemorative rather than the dynamic belief in the actual transformation of the bread and wine into the body and blood of Jesus, as Jesus himself taught it.

Thousands of different Protestant denominations and non-denominational groups have formed since that time. These denominations were generally started by someone with a vision and calling who taught a new means of relating to and worshipping God and Jesus, which appealed to certain people. People joined and helped grow these new groups. Christianity carried forward the Jewish tradition of maligning and persecuting most new groups. In keeping with this tradition, since the Jews did not agree with Jesus' practices and deemed that he was starting a new cult, they persecuted and executed him. Christianity has been equally as merciless toward virtually all their new groups. When a new group grows large enough they are eventually considered a denomination. They are then often accepted by the other major denominations, as long as the majority approves of their teachings. This acceptance as a denomination comes only after much discrediting, and then is only offered begrudgingly. If the groups stay small, the large ones tend to continue maligning them and encourage all kinds of fear and mistrust of their practices. Quakers were hung on the Boston Common. Jehovah's witnesses, Christian Scientists and Mormons, though all quite large churches now, are still greatly suspected and more or less subtly persecuted, being considered non-Christian by most mainstream Protestants. Although the large denominations such as Baptists and Methodists were called cults and mistreated by others when they were the minority, now as the majority, some of their members still tend to forget and give the same bad treatment they received when they were smaller, to other up-and-coming groups, orders and churches.

There have been times throughout history when an upwelling of spiritual interest and popular participation in alternative spiritual groups has arisen. In the late 19th and early 20th centuries, a group of new teachings was introduced to American society which has had quite an impressive influence in spiritual and religious circles ever since. Founded by Mary Baker Eddy, the Christian Science movement came into a world of conservative Protestantism and became quite influential. Emma Curtis Hopkins studied for a time with Mary Baker Eddy and then went on to found the schools of New Thought. Hopkins, in turn, taught, Charles and Myrtle Fillmore who in 1889 founded Unity School which grew and spread throughout the 20th Century, right alongside Christian Science and numerous lesser-known groups that emerged during this time. Another notable student of Hopkins' was Ernest Holmes, who founded Science of Mind, which also continues into the present time.

Many of these groups introduced concepts that were new to most Americans. Some of the teachings include reincarnation and Rosicrucianism, a mystical movement from Europe that opened up the way for teachers of the East to come into the American religious scene. The first gurus came to the United States in the late 19th century and introduced Americans, who were hungry for greater depth of meaning in their religious education, to the wisdom texts of the East and to the possibility of having spiritual teachers. Attendees at these gurus' lectures and meditation sessions heard with wonderment about high-level initiations that could lift a person into a whole other level of being. They were told of advanced individual spiritual instruction, which could transform and free a person from all their attachments and limitations into a new life of deep inner peace and loving presence. Though most people had no interest in hearing of such possibilities, a core group began to pursue such spiritual growth and form schools and organizations that offered to promote these Eastern esoteric teachings and practices.

In the early 20th century, Sigmund Freud and Carl Jung introduced the psychology of the unconscious, which brought about the beginnings of the psychotherapy movement. Though it was to be many years before the masses would accept the value of psychotherapy, eventually the concepts of introspection and the importance of addressing emotional wounds and traumas in order to heal them would be accepted. Also during this time period, Albert Einstein introduced the Theory of Relativity, bringing to the Western world the first major shift in our understanding of the physical world and how it worked since Isaac Newton pioneered this concept 150 years before. Einstein's impact on how people thought of the world around them was immense, though it also took many years for the consciousness of the general public to even begin to grasp this and allow it to sink in. Under the influence of all these exciting new ways of understanding ourselves and our material, mental, emotional and spiritual worlds, many new spiritual movements arose and with them, the teachers or leaders who led them.

One of the master teachers who came out of this time was Father Paul Blighton. He was an ordained Protestant minister and received advanced training in Sufism, Rosicrucianism, esoteric Christianity and Kriya Yoga. He took many of the benefits offered through the alternative spiritual forms coming along at this time. In 1967 he combined them and formed a holy order, which he named the Holy Order of MANS. This order had characteristics of a monastic order, but simultaneously functioned in the world. The dynamism of faith and dedication of its members was very reminiscent of the early years of Christianity. Father Paul was a dynamic spiritual teacher. He synthesized Western esotericism with the teachings and practices of early Christianity. He trained the ministers he ordained in the inner or mystical path of Christianity including the use of all seven Christian sacraments and the devotion to Mother Mary. In addition, he taught them astrology, the teachings of reincarnation, the principles of the New Thought movement, of Rosicrucianism and the benefits of true initiations and having a spiritual teacher who is trained and authorized to give such initiations. He trained and ordained several hundred priests and a number of master teachers, whom he empowered to pass on these teachings.

This order rapidly attracted many, primarily young people, who flocked in to learn of the Christian mysteries, which were joined in such a unique way with the esoteric and Eastern teachings that had become so popular during these years. In this order, students found a means to have a deeply committed spiritual life while growing and learning from priests and teachers who were trained in the path of initiations and blessings. Father Paul Blighton died in 1974, and not long thereafter the Holy Order of MANS joined the Russian Orthodox Church. Those members who did not want to become Orthodox left the group and remained on their own to choose to pursue or practice whatever they decided thereafter. I received my own introduction to the mystical Christian teachings through the Holy Order of MANS. I had been seeking a spiritual path with a spiritual teacher, such as I had read of in Autobiography of a Yogi and other books about Eastern gurus and teachers. I lived in yoga ashrams, following the yogic life practices to my highest knowing. When I found such a small amount of transformation happening in myself and the students of yoga I lived with, I wondered whether that was because we had such little exposure to any teachers in a direct one-on-one relationship.

I left the ashram and lived in a Sufi/Gurdjieff training program for a year, immersing myself in these practices with the hope of earning the right to have a Sufi teacher teach me. When the head teacher told me he was not a real teacher and that he saw my way being the Christian way, I had to overcome my resistance to Christianity. The only Christian practice I had been involved in as an adult was that of the Holy Order of MANS which was before my Sufi training. I was quite attracted to their teachings and to the light I perceived them carrying. But they were in decline by this point, and they limited how far married and parenting people could advance in their training. So this was not a viable option for my training as I wanted to go as far as possible on the spiritual path and this order had limitations based on my marriage and parenting status.

During this time period, Father Peter Bowes, who now co-directs the Order of Christ Sophia with me, was serving as a minister in the Holy Order of MANS (HOOM). He left it in 1979 when it was heading into its decline, only to be taken into personal training by one of the former HOOM master teachers, Master Raeson Ruiz. After the first six months of teaching Father Peter and seeing his student's potential to lead an order, Master Raeson moved into Father Peter's home to give him intensive ongoing training for an additional ten-month period. At the end of this time, in April of 1982, Master Raeson ordained Father Peter both as a priest and a master teacher and passed on to him the rights to train and ordain other priests and master teachers. He also passed on to him the fledgling order they were forming. Master Raeson died soon thereafter in 1983.

I met Father Peter and began working with the order he was leading in 1983, which was called the Brotherhood of Christ. I was trained for a year and a half by him. Then, while living in Massachusetts, for an additional nine years I was trained by another master teacher from that same order. This order was disbanded in 1989, though I continued my training with my teacher until 1995. In 1996, Father Peter and I reconnected and he ordained me a priest. I immensely missed all the blessings I had experienced while being a part of a holy order and a deeply mystical spiritual community. I felt guided to form such an order for women and did so immediately after receiving priest ordination and began teaching and ministering in the Boston area.

Father Peter, who lived in Milwaukee, started teaching mystical Christian classes again in 1998. In 1999, we decided to join forces and together formed the Order of Christ Sophia, for spiritual training for men and women. We took all the blessings and goodness we had learned from the Holy Order of MANS and updated and clarified their teachings. We eliminated the aspects of that order that had been troublesome and added what had been missing. As we were both psychotherapists, we greatly deepened the thoroughness of the training by expanding the use of various methods to help people heal emotional and psychological wounds while growing in their direct experience of God. We also introduced the concept and practice of learning how to relate to others in a very deep and real way as part and parcel of becoming whole and being a living, functioning part of a mystical Christian community.

This current order now is made up of and uses the best aspects of all that has come before us: The early Christian teachings and Christian community way of life. We encompass the wonderful reality and power of holy orders brought to us through Saint Francis; the great teachings, practices and initiations brought to us from the East; the important insights brought to us through the New Thought movement; the powerful understanding that came through the development of physics; and the depth of understanding of the human psyche that came through psychology. In the religious and spiritual realms, we lead in teaching the power of the divine feminine in how we work with Jesus and Mary as equals. We empower women and men to become strong and hold spiritual authority. We teach both sexes how to get in touch with their feelings while becoming more comfortable with their strength. We use memory healings and past life regressions to help our students attain wholeness and healing, and we teach devotion and prayer to open their hearts.

We also had to learn to live and grow through the criticism and hatefulness that have at times been hurled our way. We have learned to love and have compassion for those who want to harm and defame us. We understand that families no longer consider themselves blessed to have one of their members enter monastic life and join a holy order. In Ireland up until very recently, every oldest son was expected to be a priest and at least one daughter a nun. The entire family was known as blessed by the ones who took vows in service to God. Now most families want to keep their members to themselves and resent one choosing to separate from worldly and family life to live a life devoted to God. The greatest source of criticism coming our way has been that our members seem to love God and their service to God more than they love their parents and siblings. Jesus said, "Love the Lord your God with all your heart, all your mind, all your strength and all your soul. And love your neighbor as yourself." And he said,

"Truly I tell you, there is no one who has left house or brothers or sisters or mother or father or children or fields, for my sake and for the sake of the good news, who will not receive one hundredfold now in this age – houses, brothers and sisters, mothers and children, and fields with persecutions – and in the age to come eternal life."

We strive to follow the teachings of Jesus and accept that we will often not be understood or appreciated by others when we do so.

We now also understand that it is a centuries-old American tradition to assail all new religious movements with name-calling and sometimes even violence. The Christian Scientists, the Mormons, the Jehovah's Witnesses and even groups now considered mainstream, such as the Catholics, Baptists and the Methodists, were once persecuted and defamed. So we accept that this is a time-honored tradition and we are humbled to be able to experience at least a little of the persecution that Jesus and the early Christians did.

The Order of Christ Sophia holds all the great developments in human knowing and spirituality in one order; each contribution from saintly and enlightened people of the past come together in this order as individual flowers blended into a beautiful bouquet. Thanks to the long line of those who have gone before us who brought truth, sanctity, devotion and the path to enlightenment to us, we have a full and complete path to offer those who come to us and want to enter into a life of light, faith and consciousness. We are so grateful to all those who have developed and lived the way, the truth and the life and who passed it on for us to now live and give to others. We offer it to all who seek, to all who desire to enter into the deep mysteries of spiritual life, and to all who want to come to know their Creator and enter into mystical union with the God of love.

This is our history. What is to come is up to God. We wait in joyful expectation for the continued unfolding of God's will for and through this order, through the guidance of the Holy Spirit and from our beloved teachers, Jesus and Mary.

About the Author

Mother Clare Watts is an ordained Priest, Master Teacher, and Co-Director of the Order of Christ Sophia, a mystical Christian order with 13 spiritual training schools called Centers of Light. She is also a certified midwife and holds a Masters in Counseling Psychology. Prior to dedicating her life to spiritual service, she completed three years of postgraduate training in Jungian psychology and practiced both midwifery and psychotherapy for a number of years. Continually drawing from her education and her experience, including living in yoga ashrams and a Sufi school, Mother Clare has garnered a reputation for her clarity of vision. Each week she lectures in different cities on mystical Christianity and how to lead a conscious life. She has four grown children and lives in Colorado, where she oversees the development of the Sophia Peace Center. Mother Clare is the author of two books, *Giving Birth to God: A Woman's Path to Enlightenment* and *Mystical Roses of Peace*.